SMALL CRUISER NAVIGATION

SMALL CRUISER NAVIGATION

Equipment and Methods

R. M. TETLEY

David & Charles
Newton Abbot   London   North Pomfret (Vt)

British Library Cataloguing in Publication Data
Tetley, R. M.
Small cruiser navigation.
1. Navigation – Handbooks, manuals etc
I. Title
623.89   VK555
ISBN 0–7153–8520–8

Photoset by
Northern Phototypesetting Co, Bolton
and printed in Great Britain
by Biddles Ltd, Guildford, Surrey
for David & Charles (Publishers) Limited
Brunel House   Newton Abbot   Devon

Published in the United States of America
by David & Charles Inc
North Pomfret   Vermont 05053   USA

To Peg with my love and grateful thanks for her understanding and for putting up with me during a trying and difficult time   G.

Contents

1
Overcoming Time and Space Problems

Whether it be a 40,000 ton liner, a nuclear submarine, the Plymouth to Roscoff Ferry or a 22ft mini-cruiser, the navigator's primary problems are the same: where am I? What course or courses do I have to steer to get to where I want to be? The parallel does not quite end there because the basic equipment is the same despite all the modern electronic navigational aids available; it consists of a chart or charts, a compass, a log and a watch or clock. Here the parallel ends because aboard the first three types of vessel the space available to the navigator is greater than the whole deck area of a 22ft mini-cruiser, aboard which it is not possible to spread out a full-size chart with ease or comfort.

And so we come to the first of the very small cruiser navigator's problems – space, allied to which is time. Because this type of boat sails closer inshore than do her bigger sisters, there is usually less time available for the navigator to obtain a positive fix of his position, and to decide upon his next course of action. If you doubt this, try taking a round of angles, working out your position and any new course that may be necessary while you are steering the boat in a lumpy sea with a gusting wind and handling chart and instruments as well. Under these conditions time becomes very important. Remember also that you have only one hand with which to work on the chart, which is probably inconveniently folded so that the next mark on your course is on the underside. The chart will have to be refolded, and the crease smoothed out. In addition there are parallel rulers, one-handed dividers, pencils and so on to be controlled. No, a life on the ocean wave for the mini-cruiser navigator is by no means easy, and time is of the essence. Added to this problem is the fact that the resultant fix and subsequent course may well be somewhat inaccurate since working like this does not lend itself to accuracy which is of prime importance in any form of navigation, particularly in such areas as the Little Russel Channel in the Channel Islands or the Thames Estuary.

Space is the second major problem in sailing small cruisers offshore. There is nowhere aboard such a boat where a full-size chart can be spread out satisfactorily. As a result, the navigator has to fold his chart – at best a bad practice which creases the chart and can be a thundering nuisance on some later occasion when one really does want to plot a course quickly and accurately on the part which is creased. For years I have struggled with this problem of space and, in an effort to solve it, have tried out many ideas – some my own, others from people faced with the same enigma. My most recent ideas appear to have struck gold in that they have resulted in my being able to carry a chart on my knees and work on it one-handed without everything sliding off onto the cockpit floor. But the achievement of this solution has entailed a great deal of hard work on both charts and equipment.

Having established that the main problems of a small boat navigator are those of time and space, I think that it may not come amiss here to examine in very broad detail how these may be overcome, and to look at some of the background which has led up to my present thinking. My original equipment, some fifty years ago aboard a 12ft dinghy, was an old Imray, Laurie, Norrie & Wilson chart of the River Blackwater in Essex and an old 1914–18 war army prismatic compass: I had yet to learn the importance of a reliable watch. Having, in my school Officer Training Corps, learnt something of map and compass work on land, I translated my knowledge to river pilotage, and with considerable help from my father began to understand something of the yacht and small boat navigator's work. Service in the army gave me additional experience of map and compass work and I was able to expand my knowledge of navigation through having to cover long distances over large areas of almost featureless desert on my own, and having to cross this type of country at night without lights. All this is very similar to having to find one's way over the sea; map and compass course again.

Since the end of the war, I have sailed aboard many boats and was navigator on a number of them. Some were nice roomy boats with a real navigator's 'office'. Some were smaller and one had to be satisfied with a folding chart table over the navigator's bunk, or the saloon table. Smaller still and one had to fold the chart and use it on one's knees as best one could – a pursuit found to be pretty hopeless and not conducive to good results. With this experience behind me I began to bend my thought processes around this problem of space and in the fullness of time came to realise that, aboard very small cruisers, time was part of the same problem.

My first attempts to solve these two problems were directed towards creating space in some way. I very soon learnt that the old adage about quarts into pint pots was only too true. It is absolutely impossible to spread a chart anywhere aboard a small boat, where the maximum available space is only a foot or so more than the length of the chart – if that. My first attempt was to cut the charts in half and fold them round a sheet of thin plywood, but this had drawbacks; the piece of the chart which went round the edge of the ply was always, or so it seemed, just that bit which I needed for plotting a fix or Estimated Position. Also, it did not solve the problem of one-handed navigation when, as frequently happened, I was also the helmsman – navigators *per se* being a luxury known only aboard larger boats. Gradually I came to realise that not only were there the problems of time and space to be solved, but the solution had to be one which included simplicity. The simpler the equipment and methods, the easier the navigator's task would be.

At about this time I really came to appreciate, to a much greater extent than before, the qualities of the special yachting charts published by Stanford Maritime Ltd and Imray, Laurie, Norrie & Wilson Ltd, but not before I had tried my hand at reproducing charts to a suitable scale and size. Not being a hydrographic or cartographic draughtsman I found this to be too time-consuming and gave up. And then I came upon part of the answer; I would take the relevant yachting charts and cut them to a size which was suitable for use on a special chart board to be used on my knees. I decided upon dimensions which I thought were about right and started work. But the size was *not* right, it was still too large. Eventually I decided upon a standard A3 sheet which also had the advantage that, since I use traces of charts to make a record of courses sailed etc, it fitted standard-sized sheets of tracing film. The A3 size suits *me* very well; others may prefer the old Half Imperial size which is nearly as good.

I had solved the problem of space, but that of time remained. I was still trying to steer and navigate simultaneously, using one-handed dividers and a parallel rule. It was some time before I hit upon the idea of adding a pantograph to the chart board. This pantograph had to cover the entire area of the chart in use, and the straight edge had to be adjustable to all angles. Mark I was a failure. I had not been accurate enough in making it, and the locked straight edge wandered through two or three degrees between the top left-hand and bottom right-hand corners of the chart board. Mark II was an improvement, but was still inaccurate down the left-hand side, and was subjected to too much strain at the top left-hand corner. I overcame this by making a longer chart board which gave a wide margin on the left-hand side. This was Mark III, and a description of it, and of the Mark V pantograph, is given in the next chapter.

While I was experimenting with chart boards and pantographs, I was also getting suggestions and tips regarding permanent additions to charts which could result in a saving of time. From a Junior Offshore Group (JOG) navigator I learnt to draw compass roses round Marine Radio and some coastal aero beacons. This done, I found that all that was necessary, having obtained a bearing on a beacon, was to draw the back bearing from it. The saving of time which resulted from doing this was well worth that spent drawing the compass roses. A continuation of this was to draw compass roses round useful lighthouses, lightships and Lanbys. It should be obvious that these compass roses must be drawn accurately, and the method I have used is to fix the chart on the drawing board, having positioned it accurately with a T square and set square. To set up, place the set square against the T square with its vertical edge facing the left-hand edge of the drawing board. Move the chart, carefully so as not to disturb the T and set squares, until the vertical side of the latter corresponds exactly with True North on an existing compass rose or the left-hand margin of the chart. Fix the chart to the drawing board without moving anything. It is now correctly orientated to True North on the board.

Take a pair of pencil bows and draw a circle using beacon, lighthouse or whatever as centre. This circle should have a radius of about 5cm, or whatever is suitable to prevent interlocking with another rose. With a protractor, mark in Magnetic North and

12

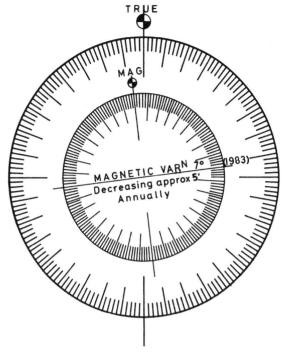

Fig 1

draw in this line. Mark in and draw the East–West line at 90° from the Magnetic North–South line. Draw another circle with a radius of 35mm and a third with a radius of 32mm. The outer circumference will give the length of the 2° graduations, and the inner that of the 10° graduations. With the protractor mark off all the 10° divisions, and draw these in in Indian ink. Do likewise for the 2° graduations, and except for adding the figures for the 10° divisions, the compass rose is complete, see Fig 1.

If it should be felt to be helpful, a True North compass rose could be drawn outside the magnetic rose, but I have found that this clutters up the chart too much and in any case a very simple addition or subtraction sum will convert a Magnetic bearing to a True one. Since Magnetic Variation only changes at the rate of about 5–8′ annually, and accurate steering aboard a small boat is seldom better than about 3°, a chart marked in this way will last for a number of years. If it is necessary to make any alterations to the charts as a result of the Admiralty Notices to Mariners, these

13

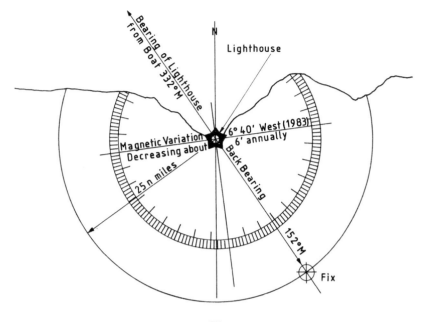

Fig 2

can be done on the Fablon covering of the chart in a self-etching mauve ink. By doing this the chart will only cease to be of use when it has worn out or faded.

In addition to the compass roses round lighthouses and lightships, I add a circle, or segment thereof, showing the maximum range of visibility of the light, allowing for my own height of eye. At night, when a known light lifts over the horizon, all that is necessary is to take a bearing on it, convert this to a back bearing (which will be explained later), mark it off on the maximum visibility radius, and lo, we have a fix, see Fig 2. There may be those who query the necessity of the outer True North compass rose, thinking that the inner Magnetic North ring should suffice. True bearings are sometimes needed, and it is occasionally necessary to convert from Magnetic to True; a dual rose saves a deal of time when this is a matter of urgency.

All the charts can now be cut to the standard A3, or Half Imperial size, irrespective of scale, since they are to be used in conjunction with the Mark V chart board. As each one is cut, a new top or bottom or vertical margin scale must be made for it since each chartlet has to be a complete unit in itself. Fig 3 shows

14

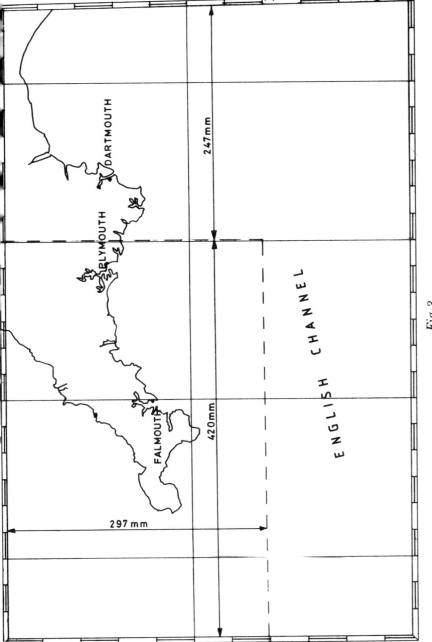

Fig 3

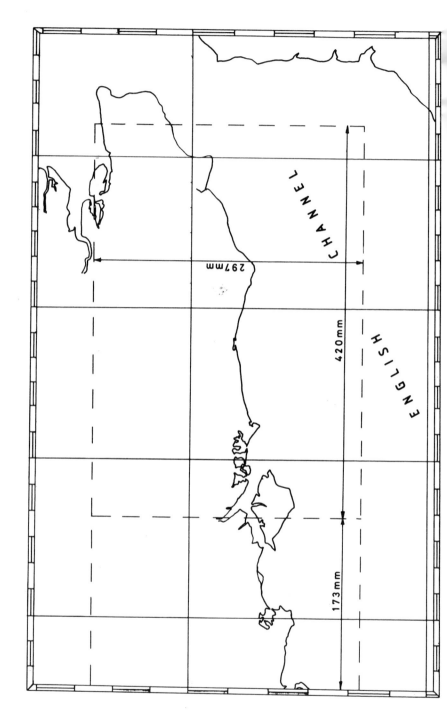

CHANNEL

ENGLISH

297mm

420mm

173mm

how the charts are dissected. Each portion is cut exactly to the required dimensions (420×297mm for A3, and 813×381mm for Half Imperial). No charts that I have met are exact multiples of the ISO 'A' Series so some of the A3 size charts have to be made up from adjacent sheets. This can produce problems, since such charts are not always to the same scale. If they are, draw a line on the next chart which coincides *exactly* with the edge of the previous one. This line *must* be True North and South – or True East and West if the charts are being prepared to cover the East or West coasts. Measure across the width of the remainder of the previous chart, and then measure across the new chart the balance needed to make up the correct A3 dimensions, see Figs 3 and 4. After the new chart portion has been cut and the new margin scale added, the two sections should make up one A3 size chart with no hiccups or misalignments where the two pieces join. When the two portions have been joined together, the cut line should be virtually invisible. As mentioned above, the trouble comes when the two adjacent charts are not to the same scale. The best way to deal with this is to end the first set of A3 charts with one which is smaller than the rest and start a new set to the new scale.

There are areas where the coast makes a change of direction of sufficient magnitude to produce problems. One of these is in the area of the Straits of Dover, another is round Land's End. Because my main chart folio begins at 50° 50′N, and 6° 35′W, I have no problems with the latter, but the Straits of Dover – although outside my normal cruising area – did present problems. I overcame these by having two cut lines, one East and West through the parallel of 51° 40′N and the other North and South along the meridian of 2° 34′W. This chart is cut from Admiralty Chart Number 1958 and is the only Admiralty Chart in my South Coast folio of passage-making charts. The next chart starts just to the north of Ramsgate, and covers the Thames Estuary. Should I want to go into one of the East Coast rivers, I change over to Imray's 'Y' Series or Stanford's Number C1. All these charts are trimmed to the A3 size for the East Coast folio.

At this stage I can almost hear readers asking how the two pieces of chart are joined together to make one A3 chart. The method I use involves waterproofing the charts at the same time with the aid of transparent Fablon. The method is simple, but requires care if the finished product is to be accurate. One sheet of the

Fablon is cut some 15mm larger all round than the chart. Since an A3 size sheet is 420×297mm and I like to have a plain white left-hand margin 150mm wide, if we now add 15mm all round we have the size to which to cut the Fablon: namely 600×327mm. A second sheet of Fablon is cut exactly the same size as the chart plus margin, ie 570×297mm. I use an old Imperial size drawing board to which is fixed a sheet of white cartridge paper. On this are drawn two rectangles corresponding exactly to the size of the Fablon sheets. Using double-sided adhesive tape, the smaller sheet of Fablon is fixed down on the drawing board over the larger rectangle, *sticky side up*. The chart is now put VERY CAREFULLY over the smaller rectangle, *face upwards*. Of course, where two parts of a chart have to be joined together, one part is fixed first, followed by the second after the mating edges have been very carefully married so that the joint is perfect. The chart is not laid flat on to the Fablon, but is rolled on so as to eliminate any air bubbles. These are worked out with a firm soft cloth which is also used to remove unwanted wrinkles.

When the chart has been fixed down onto the backing, add the 150mm wide strip of white paper on the left-hand side, not forgetting to add a margin scale to the edge of the chart should this be required. This done, the next job is to trim the Fablon exactly to the correct size (570×297mm). For this I find that a sharp model-maker's knife is ideal, used in conjunction with a steel straight edge. I place the chart face up on a sheet of thin chipboard, and press down very hard on the steel straight edge when cutting. When trimmed, the edges are absolutely true, which besides looking neat makes the next part of the job a great deal easier. The second, larger, sheet of Fablon (600×327mm) is now very carefully rolled on to the face of the chart, sticky side down, at the same time working out the wrinkles and air bubbles and keeping the edges along the lines of the larger rectangle. A vitally important factor in applying this second sheet of Fablon is that it is a once-only job, because if the Fablon is pulled away from the chart, it will take part of the printed surface with it since the adhesive is very strong.

After successfully sticking the second sheet of Fablon down onto the chart, the corners of the former are cut away, each one at an angle of 45° as in Fig 5(i). The edges of the Fablon are folded over to the back so that their ends form a perfect mitre seam, Fig 5(ii).

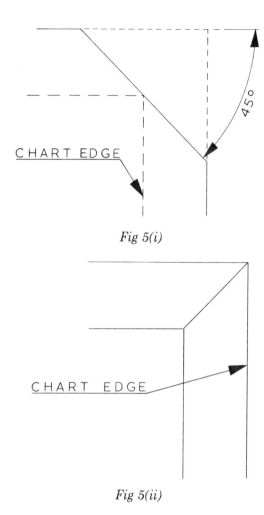

CHART EDGE

45°

Fig 5(i)

CHART EDGE

Fig 5(ii)

The waterproofing of the sheet is now complete. The need for care in every part of this operation cannot be too strongly stressed since the accuracy of the finished article is of paramount importance.

Before leaving the subject of waterproofing charts, I want to say something about those charts which are folded when bought. Many yachting charts and all Admiralty Charts are flat or rolled when purchased, but others can only be bought folded. If one tries to stick Fablon or other self-adhesive transparent film onto a folded chart, the chances are that air will become trapped in the region of the folds, and in some way unknown to me moisture finds

19

its way in and eventually turns that part of the chart brown and spoils it. The most effective method I have found for dealing with this is to iron out the creases before commencing the waterproofing operation; this is my method of doing it. I take a sheet of plywood and lay it on a table, and on to it I put one thickness of an old cotton sheet. I lay the chart *face down* on the board, and place a piece of damp blotting paper over the area of a crease, then proceed to press it with a hot iron using lots of pressure. I lift the blotting paper periodically to check on progress, and when all trace of the fold has disappeared I move on to the next crease. It is MOST IMPORTANT that the blotting paper should be damp, not wet, since wetness could well distort the face of the chart. I personally do this ironing just before putting the chart on to the Fablon backing, while some people iron out the creases before cutting the chart; both methods seem equally effective. Treating the charts in this way stops air pockets forming, and so prevents moisture from spoiling them.

Let us now look at charts in some detail. We can then work out the pros and cons of each type, of which there are three published in the United Kingdom. Admiralty Charts by the Hydrographic Office, Stanford's Coloured Charts for Coastal Navigators by Barnacle Marine Ltd and Imray, Laurie, Norrie & Wilson's 'C' and 'Y' series charts. Apart from being used for passage planning, I think that most small boat owners would agree that the majority of Admiralty Charts contain too much information, most of which is of interest to big ships only. This is not to decry them – far from it, they are the finest charts in the world – but they are just too much for the very small boat man who wants to obtain his information quickly. The Hydrographic Department are now producing charts for yachtsmen, and when they have produced a complete series I shall probably be among the first to get a set. The Admiralty Harbour Charts are of great value and, now that many of the smaller harbours are being included, it is worth making up a Harbour Chart folio for a cruising area.

I use a full-size set of Admiralty Charts to a small scale for doing all the 'dirty' work of passage planning in the early preparatory stages of a cruise so that I can draw, erase and redraw to my heart's content without making a mess of my actual navigating charts, and when I have finished planning I can erase all the markings and clean the surface with breadcrumbs, ready for use the next time.

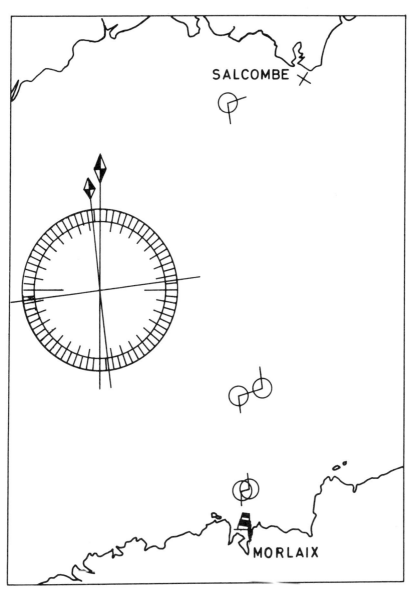

Fig 6

As an example of what I mean, when planning a windward passage from, say, Salcombe to Morlaix in North Brittany, I can work out a preliminary scheme of tacks along the plotted course, modifying where necessary, and when I am satisfied with the results I transfer the final details to traces which I can use as masters for my passage charts. This involves marking down each point at which I propose to tack, and where I intend changing from equal tacks to a long leg and a short, should this become necessary. See Fig 6, where each tack is marked, and the geographical position is entered in my navigation notebook.

Although outside my normal cruising area, there is one large-scale Admiralty Chart which I do have, and this is of the Straits of Dover. Such are the problems attendant upon crossing the traffic lanes in this area that I have found it vital to plot my actual course over the ground at frequent intervals so as to be able to make course corrections to allow for the vagaries of wind and tide which can affect the actual course sailed. Failure to obey traffic lane regulations could cost thousands of pounds and, I would add, there is no appeal against the findings of the court which imposes the fine.

My passage-making charts are all kept in folios which relate to particular cruising areas, and are a mixture of Stanford's and Imray's charts. In actual fact I have a complete set of each for the South Coast but, in the light of experience, and as a result of personal preference, I have found that a mixture provides the best coverage. It is interesting that, in my South Coast folio, each type is equally represented. I think that this shows what an excellent standard both publishers have achieved, especially so when it is realised that the second-string folio is virtually as good as the first. Both Imray and Stanford have published their coloured charts for yachtsmen for a long time, and as the years have passed they have benefited from previous experience so that the quality of their charts improves steadily year by year. The colouring is used to differentiate between land, drying mud or sand, and water, and to show the underwater contours which are most likely to be of interest to yachtsmen. Some Admiralty Charts are coloured, but as I have said before their accent is on big ships. The Harbour Plans are all coloured, and are of value to large and small alike. I think that I now have a complete set of the South Coast Harbour Plans; in many, nothing larger than a small trawler could enter, but for the small boat cruising man they are invaluable. Both Stanford and Imray produce Harbour Plans as insets on their main charts, and on their passage-making charts they frequently give large-scale inserts of difficult routes. One item I like on the Stanford charts is the harbour information which is printed on the backs of the sheets. Had it not been for the large-scale inserts and the added information on the back of Stanford's Coloured Chart No 13, I do not think that I would ever have undertaken the entrances of the rivers Erme and Avon in Devonshire.

We now come to some rather special charts, at least as far as sailing men on this side of the Channel are concerned; these are the *Cartes Guides de Navigation Cotière* (CGNC) published by Éditions Cartographiques Maritimes. They give complete coverage of the French Channel, Atlantic and Mediterranean coasts, and as far as I have been able to find out are all to the same scale of 1:50,000. They may seem a bit strange to our eyes, being used to the British style of chart, but as one grows accustomed to the presentation their value becomes apparent. As I understand it, movements are afoot to standardise conventional signs on charts throughout the world, but I have a feeling that it may be some time before this comes to pass.

The signs on the CGNC charts are more or less self-explanatory, and one idea in particular which I like very much is the way in which lighthouse information is imparted. There is no need to stare, possibly in bad light, trying to decipher the small print giving the characteristic signal and range of a lighthouse. This is shown as an arc of a circle which is divided up into white and coloured spaces representing the colour and duration of the flash, and the duration of dark. Round the circumference of this arc is printed, in large clear letters, the maximum range of the light's visibility. For every harbour there is shown the safe course or courses for entry, as well as the safest course through a difficult passage. Although printed on thinner paper than British charts the CGNC charts are waterproofed, but can still be drawn on. Although, in spite of their thinness, they are claimed to be tear-resistant – a big advance on their predecessors of ten years ago which were very flimsy and tore all too easily – they need more careful handling than the British ones if they are to last any length of time; in addition to their coastal charts, Éditions Cartographiques Maritimes publish very good Tidal Charts for the English Channel, Radio Signal Charts for all three French coasts and, above all, some really excellent maps and charts of the French Inland Waterways. There is a series of fourteen of these entitled *Cartes Guides Fluviales*, and for anyone contemplating an inland voyage through France they are ideal. I would add that they are printed in French, German and English, while the *Cartes Guides Cotières* give their information in four languages.

2
Chart Board and Pantograph Construction

The Mark V chart board itself (shown in finished form in Fig 7) is, in essence, a sheet of plywood 600×300×12mm thick. My first chart boards were made from marine-grade plywood, but only because I had some handy in the workshop. The Mark V board is made from WBP grade, and is, in fact, 13mm thick, but in every way I have found it to be perfectly adequate. My early boards were made from $\frac{3}{8}$in material but I found that this bent under certain circumstances. Consequently I have made my present board from the thicker ply which, after thorough testing, has proved to be rigid enough and the added weight has given better stability when balanced on my knees. In addition to the plywood, the Mark V board has an all-round edging of 12·5mm wide iroko (this could be mahogany); again, I happened to have some handy.

The plywood is cut, planed and sandpapered to the required dimensions, as is the edging. Two lengths of the edging are cut measuring 625mm, and another two to a length of 325mm. Mitres are cut and fitted at all the ends, and the edging is then glued and pinned to the plywood as shown in Fig 7. Use a good quality resin glue such as Cascamite or Aerolite 300, in conjunction with *brass* panel pins. Steel ones react with the acid hardeners which cause stains in the timber; in addition, should moisture penetrate the wood the pins could rust and again cause unsightly stains. For these reasons it really is not worth saving the odd penny by buying the slightly cheaper steel panel pins.

When the glue fixing the edging has set, the whole board should be sanded down, greater care being taken on the working face of the board since, when using thin paper charts such as the CGNC, grain in the timber could cause problems when working on the

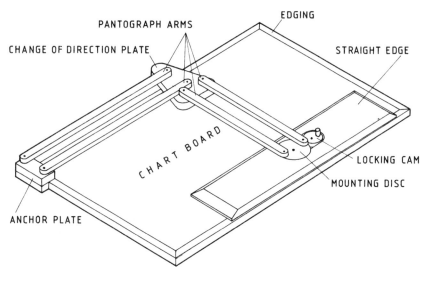

Fig 7

chart. On my present board I rubbed down first with medium two sandpaper, but one could just as easily use a medium-grit garnet paper. Because different people prefer different finishes it is a matter of preference whether the board is finished with paint or with varnish. Mine is painted a very pale duck-egg green. I first applied two coats of metallic pink primer, giving a light dry rub-down between coats using a fine-grade sandpaper. The primer was followed by four coats of white undercoat with a wet rub-down between coats using a fine-grit wet-and-dry paper. Because I had previously found that a full gloss finish was too shiny, I used a fifty-fifty mixture of undercoat and gloss for finishing. This has given a semi-matt effect which is exactly right for the job. If a varnished finish is preferred, I recommend that the last coat be flattened down with pumice powder and soft soap or a cutting-in wet-and-dry paper used wet. To finish I would use a lamb's wool bonnet on a sanding disc fitted to an electric hand drill. Finally, to prevent the board slipping off my knees, I glued some 6mm thick rubber foam onto the underside with Evo-Stick.

The Mark V chart board being now complete, work can start on the parts of the pantograph. These consist of an anchoring plate, four pantograph arms, a change of direction plate and an adjustable straight edge. As to materials, aluminium – unless a salt-water-resisting quality is obtained – corrodes too easily whilst stainless steel and brass are too heavy. There are two satisfactory materials: Perspex and good quality hardwood. I have used both Perspex and iroko for the arms, and have found both to be entirely satisfactory. I have a suspicion that Perspex could bend a bit unless the thickness of the section were to be slightly greater than that of the timber arms. If one wants to use Perspex, the parts can be made in the same way as the timber ones except that I use a super glue instead of a resin timber glue. However, acetone acts as a very good glue for Perspex, and two pieces can be cemented face to face without any loss of transparency.

One of my present Mark V pantographs is made up throughout of mahogany, including the adjustable straight edge. The anchor plate is made up from two pieces glued together as shown in Fig 9. The arms and change-of-direction disc can be made from iroko, teak or mahogany if timber is to be used, and for the plastic laminate one could use Warerite instead of Formica. The performance of all these materials is completely satisfactory since all have been tried out at one time or another. Apart from having

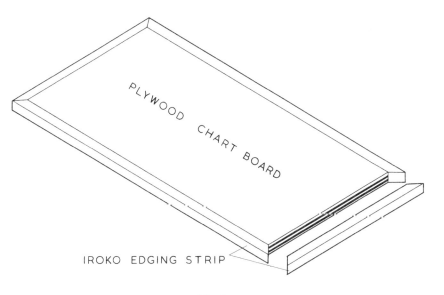

Fig 8

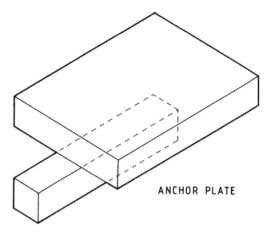

ANCHOR PLATE

Fig 9

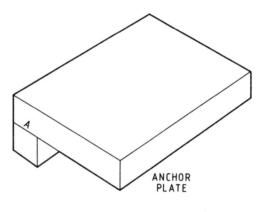

A

ANCHOR
PLATE

Fig 10

to drill all the holes very accurately, the whole assembly is very simple to make. Where the anchor plate is concerned, joint A in Fig 10 should be glued with either Cascamite or Aerolite 300. To glue the plastic laminate to the wood I used Evo-Stick which has stood up to the elements as well as anything I have ever tried. Super glue *can* be used for this, but I feel that it is a rather expensive way of doing it. I find that the laminate manufacturers recommend a latex-based adhesive, as do all the do-it-yourself experts in books and periodicals. The anchor plate is drilled and countersunk to take four 8-gauge countersunk-head screws for fixing it to the chart board; alternatively this could be glued in position, but once done it cannot be removed. Two 1mm holes are accurately drilled for the horizontal arm pivots which are round-headed brass wood screws.

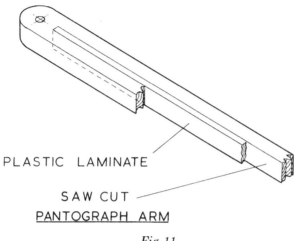

PLASTIC LAMINATE

SAW CUT

PANTOGRAPH ARM

Fig 11

The horizontal arms are made from iroko or mahogany to which is glued plastic laminate, but not before a stiffener from the same material has been inserted. To do this, make a saw cut with a coping saw along the arm, leaving a short piece at either end to allow for drilling the pivot holes. After making the saw cuts, clean up the two faces with medium-grit paper, and glue in the inserts. Fig 11 shows the saw cut and the plastic laminate insert. When the glue has set, the top and bottom surfaces of the arms are sanded down and a strip of Formica or Warerite is glued to each. To produce the desired strong connection between the inserts and the top and bottom covers of the arms, I used super glue along the top and bottom edges of the insert, and Evo-Stick on the remainder. The complete assembly now has a plastic laminate 'I' beam as shown in Fig 12, to provide longitudinal rigidity without adding too much weight.

29

All that is necessary to complete the arms is to drill the holes for the pivots. I come now to what is probably the most difficult part of making the pantograph. All the pivot holes must be drilled to within standard engineering tolerances between centres, and to prescribed limits for hole sizes. These tolerances and limits are far tighter than most do-it-yourself enthusiasts can manage, but if the completed equipment is to be to the required level of accuracy,

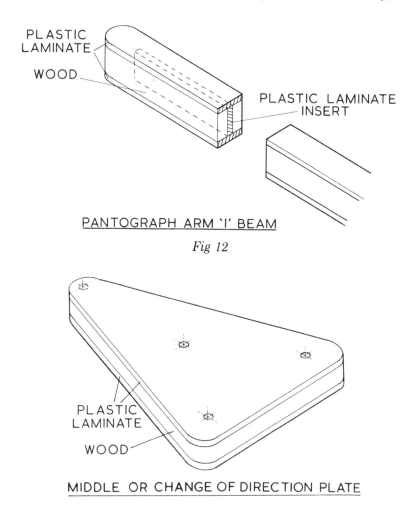

PLASTIC LAMINATE

WOOD

PLASTIC LAMINATE INSERT

PANTOGRAPH ARM 'I' BEAM

Fig 12

PLASTIC LAMINATE

WOOD

MIDDLE OR CHANGE OF DIRECTION PLATE

Fig 13

they must be adhered to, or the straight edge of the pantograph will wander through one or more degrees on any bearing, which is obviously totally unacceptable. As for the holes themselves, they must, as I have already said, be drilled to accurate limits so that there is only sufficient clearance round the screws for the arms to move smoothly on the pivots. The amount of clearance for these holes is decided by the size of the pivot screws being used. Again, unless one has a well-equipped workshop, these limits will be found to be almost impossible to meet. Therefore, when the time comes to do the drilling, the best way to overcome the problem is to take everything along to a good, reputable firm of mechanical engineers or toolmakers. Since I was not equipped to cope with these close limits and tolerances, I went to a firm of toolmakers I knew and got them to make me a drilling jig so that I could drill to the required tolerances between centres, and to prescribed limits for the hole sizes. In the latter case I bought some rather expensive drills which meant that I could drill exactly to the size I wanted. In this way, since I had more than one pantograph to make up, I could guarantee that the desired level of accuracy was always maintained.

The middle, or change-of-direction disc, is made from a piece of iroko with plastic laminate on both faces. The easiest way to make it is to glue the laminate onto the wood before cutting out the shape which, when finished, should be as in Fig 13. Four pivot pins are fitted to this, and the tolerances on dimensions are to be to the same accuracy as for the arms as described in the previous paragraph. The complete assembly of anchor plate, change-of-direction plate and mounting disc is shown as an isometric perspective in Fig 14.

The straight edge, the assembly of which is shown in Fig 23 on page 42, is somewhat more complicated to make, but should be well within the capabilities of anyone who can use tools fairly competently. The assembly can be made from either timber or Perspex. I have to admit that I sometimes experience difficulty in seeing the edge of a Perspex straight edge at night, but this may well be attributable to my poor eyesight and the fact that I use a red chart light so as not to spoil my night vision. As I have not yet met anyone else who has experienced the same difficulty, I intend to describe both types although there is no great difference between the two. My straight edge is made of mahogany, well-

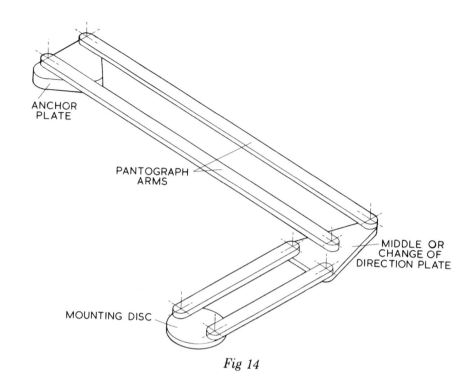

ANCHOR
PLATE

PANTOGRAPH
ARMS

MIDDLE OR
CHANGE OF
DIRECTION PLATE

MOUNTING DISC

Fig 14

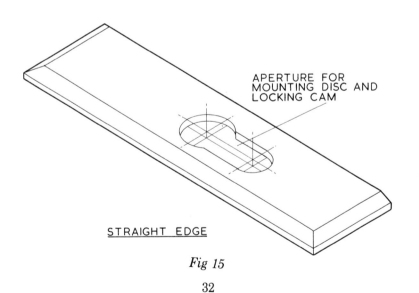

APERTURE FOR
MOUNTING DISC AND
LOCKING CAM

STRAIGHT EDGE

Fig 15

32

seasoned Honduras for freedom from warping or twisting. Also, since Honduras mahogany does not have the interlocked grain of the so-called West African mahoganies, it is very much easier to work. If Honduras mahogany is not available I would suggest teak or iroko as the next best, but be sure that the latter is brown and not yellow as yellow iroko has not been fully seasoned, and so could twist or warp.

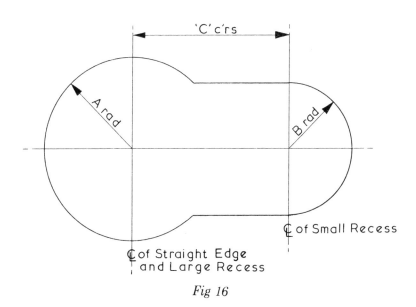

Fig 16

After cutting out the straight edge from a piece 8mm thick, the apertures for the mounting disc and locking cam have to be marked out. As can be seen in Fig 15, this aperture is more or less keyhole shaped. To mark it out, first find the exact centre of the straight edge, which is also the centre of the mounting disc, and draw a circle (radius A) on this centre. Another point (distance C) is marked along the longitudinal centre line, and a circle of smaller radius (radius B) than the first is drawn. Tangents from the smaller circle are drawn parallel to the longitudinal centre line, and these cut the larger circle as shown in Fig 16.

33

There are two methods of cutting the aperture; first by using a side-and-end-cutting milling cutter in a woodworker's router, or in an electric hand drill. This method requires some care, and the best way is to fix the electric drill into a drill stand, and the work into a clamp firmly fixed down on to the base of the drill stand. The trouble with a routing machine is that it requires a very steady hand and experience in use. Having fitted up the drill and workpiece, very carefully cut the smaller circle by cutting down on to the top tangent line to the depth of the locking cam, and then move the work slowly and carefully to the left, making sure that the milling cutter does not go over the boundary line of the aperture. Eventually a point will be reached when the miller is cutting close to the circumference of the small circle. STOP! Now go back to the beginning and start cutting along the lower tangent line, and repeat until the circumference of the small circle is again reached. By careful manipulation of the cutter the spare that is left in the small circle can be removed. To cut out the large circle, start at point A in Fig 17, and cut round the circumference, taking

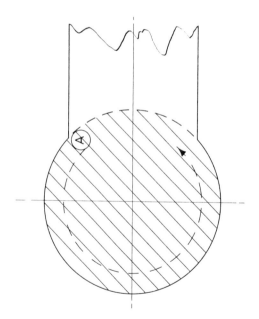

Fig 17

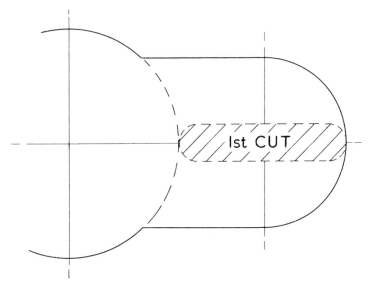

Fig 18(i)

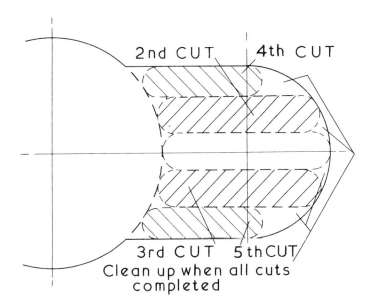

Fig 18(ii)

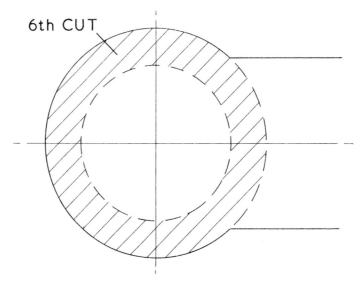

Fig 18(iii)

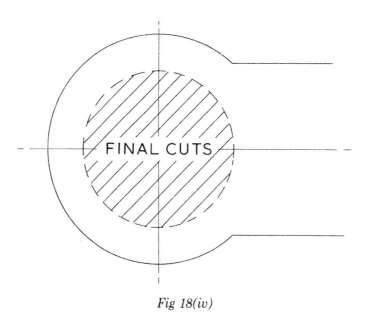

Fig 18(iv)

36

care not to go over the boundary line, until the whole circle has been cut out to the depth of the mounting disc. Any spare in the middle can now be removed; the aperture is complete and should not need any cleaning up if the job has been done carefully. These wood-milling cutters leave a very smooth finish when used correctly, and it is always better to go too slowly than too fast. The sequence for milling out this aperture is shown in Fig 18.

The second method of cutting out is more suitable for the do-it-yourself person, but it means that the original thickness of the straight edge material will have to be 5mm instead of 9mm. In fact, this helps to make the job a little easier as the tool to be used is a coping saw. It does take a bit longer, and is more tedious because the finished edge has to be cleaned up with a fine-cut, half-round file about 20cm long. This cleaning up has to be done very carefully as the edges have to finish square and true. A piece of 4mm plywood is now cut to the same shape as the straight edge. The two discs, the mounting disc and the cam, are cut to diameters 1mm less than those of the holes on the adjustable straight edge. These discs must be perfectly circular, and the sides must be finished square and as smooth as possible since they both have to rotate without hindrance. Some time after I made the

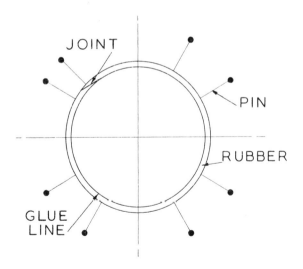

Fig 19

Mark V pantograph, I took out the locking cam and reduced it by just over 1mm on the diameter, and then stuck a slightly stretched rubber band to it. Afterwards I reassembled the whole thing and found that the modified cam worked very much better. Anyone wishing to copy this idea may find it a bit tricky to keep the rubber band in position while the glue is setting, since it is in tension and tries to slip off the edge of the disc. I held the band in position with about eight model-maker's pins as shown in Fig 19.

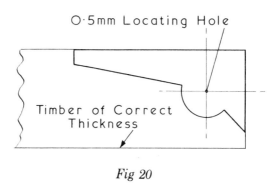

Fig 20

The next step in making up the adjustable straight edge is to make the 'ears' should these be needed. My first straight edge had them and I have to admit that I found them very useful when it came to drawing vertical or near vertical lines on a chart. However, they do add to the complexity of the job and to anyone who is not too sure about their skill of hand I would advise doing without them. The first thing to do is to draw out the 'ears' on to timber of the same thickness as the straight edge as shown in Fig 20. One is as shown, and the other is the same in reverse and if one has a small band saw both can be cut out together, and then one can be turned over. They must be very carefully cut out and equally carefully finished (a fine file is best). When they have been made, each 'ear' is placed accurately on the corner to which it is to be fitted, and its outline drawn with a fine-pointed pencil. A full circle is drawn to the same radius as the part circle on the 'ear', shown in Fig 21. This is where very considerable care has to be

taken, as the centres of the circles control the accurate continuation of the straight edge with the 'ears' in both positions.
The way I achieved this accuracy was to locate the 'ears' exactly in
position using a dial micrometer in two positions at right angles to
one another, having first fixed the workpiece into the clamp on the
drill stand. Then, having fitted a 0·5mm (0·0127in) drill into the
drill chuck, I located this with the dial micrometer. The straight
edge, 'ear' and drill thus aligned, the hole was drilled with the
knowledge that when I came to put in the pivot pin, the 'ears'
would be positioned exactly as they should, and the trueness of the
ruling edge would be correct for both positions. I next put the piece
of ply which I had cut out into position and, using the pilot hole
already drilled, continued it on into the ply. The next part of the
job was to cut out the circle in the straight edge. This again has to
be done very carefully, and the cut edge remaining must be
finished square and smooth with a fine half-round file.

The plywood base for the straight edge now has to be glued into
position using a synthetic resin glue. Prior to drilling the pilot

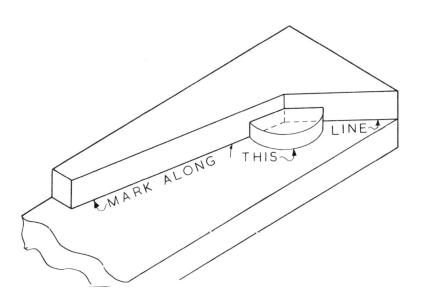

Fig 21

holes in the ply, it is most essential to use some locating pins, not less than three, so that when the gluing is taking place the ply will be accurately located in relation to the straight edge, and thus the pivot holes for the 'ears' will be correctly lined up. One other item requires careful attention; the 45° angles cut in the ends of the straight edge and on the 'ears' have to be individually fitted so that, in the vertical position, the drawing edge on the latter is at precisely 90° to the horizontal edge of the straight edge. I used a diemaker's file for this as it has a very fine cut, and one is able to make the most minute alterations, even in wood.

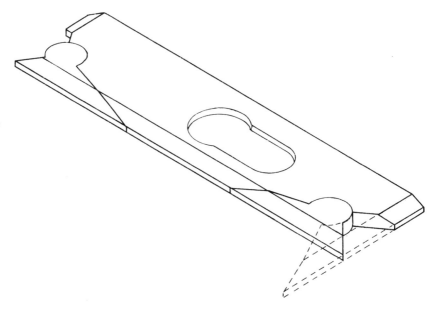

Fig 22

The pivot for the 'ears' is more effective if it is slightly larger than the other pivots because, as will be explained, it is subject to some tension. In order to hold the 'ears' in position, it is necessary to have a spring which maintains a tension in whichever position the 'ears' may be, and this spring must also be corrosion-proof. After some trial and considerable error, I found that the most satisfactory material was the yachtsman's best friend: phosphor bronze. The final choice of spring was 6·5mm (0·25in) in diameter with seven turns of 0·711mm (22swg) diameter wire giving a rate of 1.9437kgf/cm or 4.2851bf/in. This spring is strong enough to hold the 'ears' in their correct position, but not so strong as to make it difficult to operate them when conditions aren't so good.

The methods I have described were the best I could think of to obtain the accuracy I wanted. After all, if one is going to work on a chart to the closest limits of accuracy possible, these can only be as good as the equipment in use will allow; hence the care needed to make the whole assembly. The completed assembly for the straight edge is shown in Fig 22.

As I said earlier, the adjustable straight edge can be made of Perspex. The general principle in the making of it is the same as for wood, but the tools used must be those for metal working. This puts the material beyond the scope of many do-it-yourself enthusiasts. Nonetheless, for those who have access to these tools and can use them, Perspex is a very rewarding material to work, and the results are probably better than those for a wooden straight edge. After Perspex has been cut or shaped, it may require polishing to re-establish its transparency. As a case in point, the bevel along the edges of the straight edge must be transparent if any advantage is to be gained from using the material. This, in fact, is the only time that a woodworking tool is used, and this is the hand plane with a very sharp iron set fine. The best way of polishing Perspex that I have found is to begin by rubbing it smooth with, if you can get it, pulverised pumice powder. This is best mixed with soft soap and rubbed on with a damp soft cloth, using a tight circular motion, but don't apply too much pressure. The next stage is to treat the area with a milder abrasive, and for this I have found that Eucryl Smoker's Tooth Powder is just right. The tooth powder is also applied with a soft damp cloth, and again with a tight circular motion. To follow this, use a mixture of tooth powder and metal polish; at first the mixture should be a paste with only a little metal polish, but gradually increase the amount of the latter and decrease the amount of the former until you are using just metal polish. This polishing process is very slow and lengthy, and after the pure-metal-polish stage is reached there is still a great deal of polishing to do until the perfect surface is achieved. Finally, on the subject of Perspex, treat this material

41

with the greatest respect. It does not like being hit or jarred. Also, when using a woodworking plane on the bevelled edges, make the strokes with the tool firm and continuous; *don't stop half-way.*

With my first Mark V pantograph I made a lot of mistakes. Firstly, I did not pay enough attention to the tolerances of the various parts and secondly I was not particular enough about the limits and fits for the pivots and their holes. The result was an equipment which was far too sloppy, resulting in unacceptable inaccuracies. I had to make the whole thing again, but this time I used far more care. I then succeeded in gumming up a part of the straight edge pivot, and from this I learnt to use the very minimum amount of glue, and to apply it very carefully to those areas where it was needed *and nowhere else.* The final edition of the pantograph took rather a longer time to make, but amply repaid the extra care involved. The present assembly is

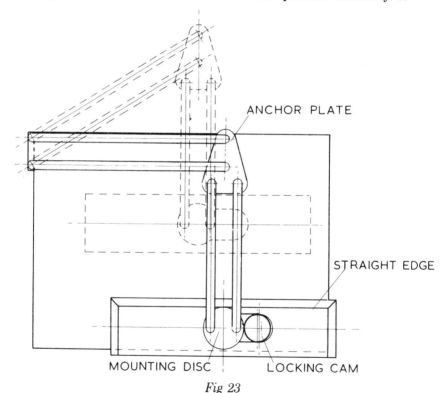

Fig 23

beautifully smooth in operation and is accurate. The completed chart board and pantograph are shown in Fig 23.

There are one or two useful tips for those who want to make their own pantograph and chart board. Wherever possible I glued up my assemblies using model-maker's cramps. Where, for one reason or another, I could not use cramps I utilised brass panel pins as locators. Where parts of an assembly needed small but nonetheless positive clearances, such as between the arms of the pantograph, I cut spacers from drawing paper, waxed them with candle grease to act as a lubricant, and put them between the pieces to be separated. Once the assembly was complete, I tore out the paper and found that I had just the clearance I wanted.

The subject of pivots needs, I think, a little more discussion. Where machine screws are used, I seem to have used nothing but 6BA, and all made of brass. One point about which I was very careful was to ensure that the screws were not threaded all the way up. By doing this I was able to glue them into their holes, thereby steadying them and keeping the pivot rigid. For this purpose I used super glue. One important point when using any of the epoxy or similar glues is to degrease the metal properly. Among the better degreasing agents are trichlorethylene, carbon tetrachloride and surgical spirit, but failing these methylated spirit can be used. I placed all metal parts in a coffee jar into which I poured trichlorethylene, then screwed on the lid. As I required the pieces, I took them out of the jar and placed them in a tray of the degreasing agent, scrubbing them with an old toothbrush. Once degreased, I never touched them with bare fingers, but held them with small long-nosed pliers so that no body grease could be transferred to them. One final, but very important, word about using degreasing agents such as those I have named: always use them in the open air, or make certain that there is a good circulation of air if using them indoors. These agents are very volatile, and if the fumes from them are inhaled, they could harm your health.

After I had been using the chart board and pantograph for some while, I added some phosphor-bronze spring clips to the bottom left-hand corner of the board to hold pencils. Some people prefer to use a pencil case or holder of some kind, but because Chinagraph pencils can break rather easily, and a replacement is usually wanted in a hurry, I prefer to take one from a clip on the board.

43

These clips are fixed with 6-gauge countersunk-head wood screws. An alternative which is attractive in that it is less expensive is to fit a series of loops made either of sail cloth or Pirelli webbing. All that is needed after the clips or loops have been fitted is to slip in the pencils, where they will be firmly held until needed.

3
Additional Equipment

In the previous chapters I have written about the basic navigation equipment needed aboard any boat or ship. Even very small cruisers need something more, even though they may only hop along the coast from harbour to harbour. Whilst the ordinary passage-making charts will show how to get from one harbour to another, a pilot's guide will tell you how to get in to your destination, where to anchor or tie up, and where to get water, fuel and supplies. Charts do not give tidal information in the form of tables of high and low water on a particular date, neither do they give high and low water levels. For this information, one must have a nautical almanac which is, in addition, a mine of information for the navigator, giving speed tables and distance off tables, together with a great deal of celestial navigation and other information. I use the *Macmillan Silk Cut Nautical Almanac*, and find that it gives me all the information I need, besides the great pleasure I get from just browsing through it. For planning a cruise, it is invaluable. I have heard it said that the book is too expensive, but I do not know where the same amount of information could be obtained for less money. *Brown's* and *Reed's Almanacs* are similar publications of really excellent quality, and as a boy I was rarely without one or the other because they made such fascinating reading. In all fairness I have to add that both books are published more with big ships in mind, and they do not contain the wealth of harbour information to be found in *Macmillan*.

Although not a nautical almanac, *The Cruising Association Handbook* – having been compiled by cruising yachtsmen for cruising men – recommends itself to the small boat fraternity. The wealth of information culled from members of the Cruising Association is enormous, and covers the whole of the British Isles and continental waters from the southern end of the Baltic to as far south as Gibraltar. It undoubtedly covers all waters available to mini-cruisers sailing out of British ports. For those who sail on the South Coast, *The South England Pilot* by Robin Brandon, published by Imray, Laurie, Norrie & Wilson, is the most convenient guide, and gives a very comprehensive coverage of the region. Volumes III, IV and V are already published, and cover from Hengistbury Head to the Isles of Scilly. Volume III extends from Hengistbury Head to Start Point, Volume IV covers the coast from Start Point to Land's End while Volume V is devoted to the Isles of Scilly. The two remaining volumes will cover from the North Foreland to Selsey Bill, and from Selsey Bill to Hengistbury Head respectively. Though the wrong size and shape for the small cruiser's bookshelf, all five volumes can be very conveniently stowed flat under the bunk cushions (navigator's bunk!). Again the price might seem high, but when the amount and quality of the information contained are considered, their cost appears in a very different light. *The Pilot's Guide to the East Coast of England* by Derek Bowskill covers the region from the south shore of the Thames Estuary to the Wash, an area which presents some of the best pilotage problems to be found round our coasts. For those whose taste for adventure leads them across the North Sea or the English Channel, there is an abundance of pilot's guides by such well-known authorities as K. Adlard Coles whose *North Brittany Pilot* is a must for anyone cruising those waters, and Mark Brackenbury whose *Frisian Pilot* is not only essential for cruising the region, but also makes very good reading on its own account. Edward Delmar Morgan's *Normandy Harbours and Pilotage* is another essential for that particular area.

All these books are of a suitable size to fit into a small cruiser's bookshelf. There are many more excellent publications but since a small boat's bookshelf is of limited size the owner has to make a decision regarding its contents, bearing in mind that there must be room for instruction manuals for the engine and any other mechanical, electrical or electronic equipment. These must be carried and kept in polythene bags to keep them dry for when they are needed.

One more important book for the navigator's collection is on weather forecasting, since much of his skill lies in being able to foretell, in so far as is possible, changes which might affect his plans, and taking advantage of them quickly. Just such a book is Ray Sanderson's *Meteorology at Sea.* This is a most comprehensive coverage of the subject. In my opinion, it is not only the racing navigator whose plans are affected by the weather; a good fast sail from one port to another is just as desirable for the cruising man.

The bookshelf itself needs to be in a dry part of the boat, and so arranged that a bar or fiddle can be fitted across it to prevent everything spilling out when the going gets rough. Under these conditions, when there may well be water slopping over the cabin sole, there are few more exasperating things than to find the pilot's guide or nautical almanac soaking wet with all the pages stuck together, just when they are most needed. I know – I learnt the hard way! I advise a piece of shock cord or bunjie being fixed horizontally round the books, and another piece vertically across the tops. In this way everything is fixed firmly into the shelf, no matter what the boat does; see Fig 24. In the past, I have been surprised at the number of small boat owners who seem to think that books can be quite safely left in kit nets under the deck head. There are even those who think that books are not necessary and seem quite happy to attempt to enter unknown harbours 'by guess and by God'; some of these have stubbed their toes on rocks and others have needed to be hauled off sandbanks. The amazing thing is that in spite of experiences of this type they do not seem to learn. Pilot's guides and nautical almanacs are essential to navigators; just as essential as charts.

The best navigator is only as good as his equipment and its accuracy will allow. For this reason, one should always buy the best that finance permits, although it must be said that expensive does not always mean good. The best way in which to find out about the quality of different instruments is to talk to people with experience in their use, and take advantage of their knowledge in making a choice. I said earlier in this book that the navigator's basic tools are chart, log and compass. A compass is worse than useless, it is actively dangerous, if it has not been correctly swung so that its deviation on all points of sailing is known. In any case of doubt, call in a qualified compass adjuster; his fee will be amply repaid by the peace of mind gained from the knowledge that the compass can be relied upon at all times. And on the subject of compasses, do site them so that the helmsman can view the card without having to crane his neck this way or that in order to be able to see it. That way lies unnecessary helmsman fatigue which in turn leads to errors in steering which could lead to disaster. A fully corrected compass with a proper deviation card is a must, and every navigator should insist on the deviation card being sited where he can see it when at work. And while on the subject of compass cards, for small boats I recommend a domed-type compass with three lubber lines; one on the fore and aft line with one on either side at about 45° so that the helmsman can steer a course from either side, adjusting the compass reading to suit.

The navigator's second basic tool is the chart, and I have already dealt with this, so we can get on to the third item which is the log. Again, if this cannot be relied upon it is, like an unswung compass, worse than useless. It is the duty of every cruising owner to check his log under as many conditions of wind and sea as

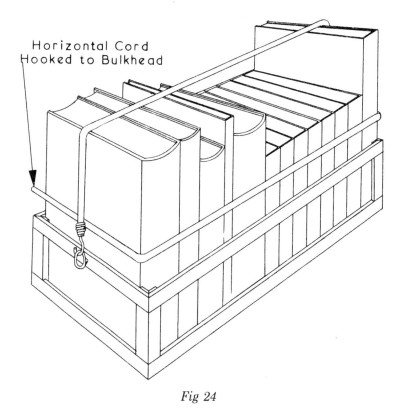

Horizontal Cord
Hooked to Bulkhead

Fig 24

possible, as well as on all points of sailing so that its characteristics shall be thoroughly known. An example of what I mean is when, beating to windward in a big sea, the log would probably over-read, and it is by how much it over-reads that is important. Speed also can affect the performance of a towed log spinner (so can sharks!); if the boat is travelling really fast, the spinner will come near the surface and jump clear from time to time, thus under-reading. With a well-designed log, the combination of spinner and sinker weight should take care of this, but some small cruisers will plane very fast indeed downwind, and even the best of spinners will jump clear from time to time.

Paddle-wheel and doppler-type logs are very much more efficient when sited correctly, but even they can give false readings from time to time and of course they are more expensive. Another point about logs is that, in so far as my experience goes, different types perform better or worse according to hull shape, and whether or not they have been correctly sited. So it all adds up to the individual owner getting the best from his boat's particular log. It must also be realised that the log gives distance run through the water and not over the ground, so that tide and surface drift can well have an effect upon readings.

A refinement of the log, of whatever type, is the log/speedometer. Not only does this tell the helmsman whether he is getting the best speed out of the boat, but if speedo readings are recorded on the deck log every quarter of an hour it also gives the navigator an additional check on distance run over a one-or two-hour period; and I cannot stress too strongly the value to the navigator in having two or more ways of checking his calculations. It may increase his work load, but information from one source showing up an error from another is of the greatest help in working up an Estimated Position (EP), as well as adding to peace of mind which, as every navigator knows, leads to contentment for all on board and increases his own personal efficiency.

Many people would say that it is perfectly obvious that a watch is an essential piece of navigation equipment, and this is so. But how good a watch? The best that one can afford is the answer. In these days of quartz watches I would even say buy one that is *more* than you can really afford, and make certain that it is water-resistant at least. My watch is a Seiko Chronograph, and over the time that I have had it, I have been able to work out its rate so that

49

when working a position line from sun sights I can use it with complete confidence as a chronometer. Although it is water-resistant, I take very great care not to get it wet. With watches of this type it is very important to keep a record of the date when the battery is due for replacement. The battery for my watch lasts two years, so I keep a note of the date when it was last purchased. I must admit that I find the digital read-out, which can be illuminated at night, preferable to two hands which can be difficult to read even by torchlight.

On the subject of torches, I recommend that at least two be carried on board: one small torch of the pen type with the bulb coloured red, and a big powerful one for use as a searchlight when required. My small torch is an Ever Ready pen torch, and I have covered the bulb with red cellophane paper from a sweet wrapping. This is ideal for chart reading at night since it does not destroy night vision to the same extent as would a normal white light, and at the same time it provides enough light to enable the chart to be read.

The skipper/navigator/helmsman usually only has one hand free for chart work, even with the Mark V chart board. For this reason, I consider a pair of one-handed dividers to be indispensable, and would add that it is essential to learn to use them equally well with either hand. Problems can arise if you have to change hands to use the dividers; you finish up with crossed hands, and can get into a fearful tangle.

No cruiser should ever put to sea without a deck log. On this the helmsman enters, once every quarter of an hour, the *actual* course he is steering, boat speed if equipped with a speedometer, log reading and any alterations of course caused by shipping and the like. The helmsman *must* be honest about the course sailed at the time of entry. After all, no one is going to bite off his ears if he was a degree or two off; he may not have been able to help it, and the man has yet to be found who can sail a small boat to within less than 3° of a given course. At the top of the deck log should be written the course to be steered, time at which course is to be altered, the new course to be steered, and the time at which the navigator is to be called. Down the right-hand side there should be a column for any additional remarks which may be of use to the navigator when he is working up his EP. My deck log is as shown in Fig 25. The importance of the deck log is that it gives the navigator a running account of what the boat has been doing since the last time he plotted an EP, and from it he can work out the Estimated Course (EC) and so produce an EP. I have found it very useful if the helmsman enters such details as wind speed and direction, sea state, and when he altered course for shipping and for how long before he came back on to his proper course. Once every hour or two hours, the navigator transfers the deck log information into his navigation log, then wipes the deck log clean so that the helmsman can start again. In estimating course and position the deck log plays a very important part in the navigator's work.

So far I have dealt with the very basic equipment required for small cruiser navigation. Anyone who reads the yachting journals will realise the mass of electronic equipment and navigation aids available. However, it has to be said that a great deal of this is beyond the purse of small boat owners, but there are some items which can be afforded, and I intend dealing with these. First amongst them I would put echo sounders. Most small cruisers spend a good deal of their time sailing on estuaries, and an echo sounder for this type of sailing is invaluable, as it is in fog, since one can navigate by comparing the contours of the sea-bed as shown on the chart with information from the echo sounder. It is also of considerable assistance when tacking along an unknown channel in areas such as the Thames Estuary or the Wash. With care, and more importantly with experience, it is possible to survey areas where there is little or no information to be obtained from charts or pilot's guides. However, this does require an additional transducer to be fitted aboard the dinghy unless, like mine, the boat is of very shallow draught with a centreboard. This type of work is fascinating and can be of future use to others, but it calls for care and precision.

Among the lower-priced echo sounders, I have used the Seafarer for a number of years now, and can only say how valuable it has been. It has failed only twice: once when I forgot to renew the batteries, and the second time when the transducer lead came out of the set. In other words, both times the fault was mine.

Proper maintenance is the secret of ensuring reliability in any item of electronic equipment, not just echo sounders. By 'proper maintenance' I mean that the set must be treated carefully, not left aboard during the winter with the old batteries still connected. These *must* be taken out and thrown away, the set

YACHT	Denebola

DECK LOG

Course   °C until   hrs

Then change to   °C

CALL ME AT   hrs*

TIME	COURSE	LOG	REMARKS

*SEE BACK OF DECK LOG

FRONT

Fig 25

CHANGES OF COURSE

TIME	FROM	TO	REASON

MARKS, LIGHTS, ETC

NAME	INFO	ACTION

CALL ME IF/WHEN:

BACK

taken home and stored – in its original box if possible – in a cool, dry place. It should also be returned to the manufacturers at least once every two years for servicing. The reason for taking out the old batteries is that, if left in the set, they will almost inevitably run down at which point they will weep acid and cause very damaging corrosion inside the set, which could very well ruin it. Servicing, and this applies to all marine electronic equipment, is vital if the item in question is to continue to function efficiently every season, all season long.

There are a number of reasonably priced echo sounders on the market and, since the proof of the pudding is in the eating and these brands have been on the market for some time, they have proved their quality. But do buy a set of known make. The reason that I mention the Seafarer range is that I have known it and owned one for some years, and have learnt to use it correctly. I have been shipmates with other equally good makes, but was very amused once aboard a boat which was fitted with a very expensive foreign-made set – it jumped about all over the place with the boat's motion and required some fairly skilful interpolation to get anything like a reasonable reading from it. Also, the dial was not very easy to read. There is more information about echo sounders in Chapter 5.

I suppose that one of the biggest innovations in small boat equipment has been the hand-held radio direction finder (RDF). I remember that before the 1939–45 war about the most compact radio direction finding equipment was made by the Marconi Company. It was of comparable size to a present-day MF/RT set, with a large loop aerial on deck which always seemed to be getting in the way. It was a very efficient set, mind you, and I was amazed at its accuracy. Today, the hand-held RDF sets such as the Brookes & Gatehouse Homer and Heron, and the Seafix range are as good as anything one can get anywhere.

There are now so many radio beacons round the coasts of the United Kingdom and on the continent of Europe that it would be difficult to find an area where one cannot pick up at least three such stations. However, care has to be taken in the time and selection of beacons. This is because for about an hour before and after sunrise and sunset the 'nul' could give a false bearing. Also, a radio signal passing over land behaves rather like a beam of light travelling through water or glass. If light enters either medium at an acute angle it is refracted, and the amount of refraction reduces with the angle of incidence of the light beam, see Fig 26. So with a radio signal: if it crosses the coast at an acute angle it is bent quite considerably, and as the angle reduces so the amount of 'refraction' reduces. So, wherever possible, use beacons whose beams travel only over water, or which cross a coastline at right angles. I was once caught out through using the Round Island Beacon with the Land's End peninsula between us, and decided as a result that my EP was nearly ten miles away from my actual

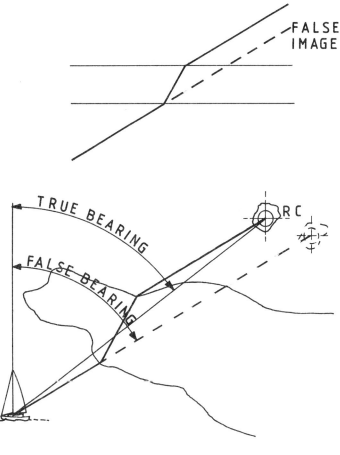

Fig 26

position. Until I learnt the errors of my ways, I used to be led astray by using the RDF set too close to sunrise and sunset. Basically, RDF works by taking bearings on a series (usually three) of beacons of known geographical position. The bearing obtained is that of the beacon FROM the boat, and the navigator wants the bearing TO the boat from the beacon. To deduce this he must add or subtract 180° depending upon whether the original bearing is smaller or greater than 180°; if smaller he adds, if greater he subtracts. The result is known as a back bearing or the reciprocal bearing from the beacon. Thus, if St Catherine's Point Radio Beacon bears 315°M, the back bearing is 315 – 180 = 135°M, so the boat bears 135°M from St Catherine's Point. If Cap d'Antifer bears 109°M, then the back bearing is 109+180 = 289°M, see Fig 27.

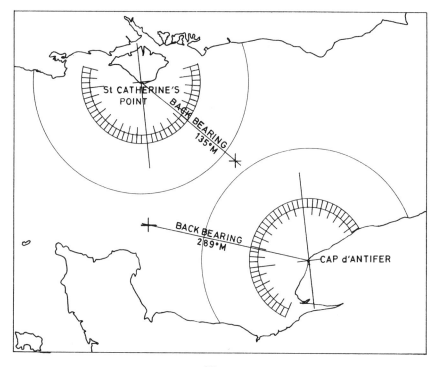

Fig 27

A very important point to watch for with a hand-held RDF set is that its compass is swung as is the steering compass, and that the set is always used with the operator standing in the same position. There should be a deviation card for the RDF set's compass, and this will have been produced with the set in a particular position; any movement away from there might be towards an item of the boat's equipment or rigging which could alter the deviation by enough to give an erroneous fix. In addition, it is important to make sure that there are no ferrous metal objects such as knives, winch handles, beer cans, etc nearby when the RDF set is in use. Items such as these can cause quite serious deviation which at best would produce a fix which was completely false, and at worst could cause disaster. On one occasion I was showing someone how to use a hand-held RDF set, and the bearings he was obtaining were totally at variance with mine. Eventually I found that he was carrying a knife in the kangaroo pocket of his sailing smock! I even take off my glasses when using either an RDF set or a hand-bearing compass since they can have quite a measurable effect on a compass needle. Another point to note is not to use the RDF set too near the boat's steering compass; they can interact with each other. For this reason also, the RDF set should be stowed well away from the steering compass (not less than five feet).

There are sophisticated RDF sets which give all kinds of digital read-outs, but providing that the small boat navigator is a person of sound common sense, this facility is not vital. What is vital is to know the Morse Code, the frequency of the beacon being sought, and its mode and sequence. It is no earthly use searching for the Outer Gabbard Light Vessel at ten past nine in the morning, because it broadcasts at nine and fifteen minutes past the hour; refer to the nautical almanacs. Also, should the set be equipped with a beat frequency oscillator (BFO) and since the Outer Gabbard Lightship's mode is A2*, then the BFO must be switched off for identification purposes. When identification has been made it can be switched back on or left off as the operator prefers.

All the necessary information regarding radio beacons is obtainable from the nautical almanacs. Full details of all beacons in the area of a cruise should be entered in the navigator's notebook. As the cruise proceeds, those which can be used on a particular day should be entered in the white space at the left-hand side of the chart. The characteristics of each beacon should be entered so that no time is wasted in looking them up.

One further comment on the subject of hand-held RDF sets: don't, just because your first few efforts with the set are not very successful, condemn the set out of hand as being inaccurate and useless. As with all other aspects of pilotage and navigation, real accuracy only comes with practice. It is vital that the small cruiser navigator gets to know his equipment, especially electronic equipment, really well so that he understands any peculiarities it may possess. I remember once, in the early days of small RDF sets aboard yachts, a man with far more money than sense trying out a new set. The results of his first effort produced what must have been one of the biggest cocked hats on record. 'This thing is no bloody use' was his assessment and, believe it or not, he threw it overboard! I was just too late to catch it. It was not that the equipment was no use; the fault was lack of patience on the part of the user and his failure to understand that such equipment needs practice in order to produce the desired results; two attributes which are essential for the navigator of any yacht, irrespective of size. A good example of this was the late Sir Francis Chichester. If his sun sights produced a 'pig's breakfast' of a position he would go back to the beginning and check every figure in every step of his calculations until he found the error. There is more information about RDF sets in Chapter 5.

So far I have dealt with out-and-out navigation equipment. There are other items which can be of great assistance to the navigator, one of them being a radio. No cruising boat, no matter what her size, should ever be without a radio receiver of proven reliability. It is difficult to be precise about transistorised radio sets because the variety is so enormous, but a reasonably small set which covers the broadcast, aircraft and marine bands is not very expensive, and many types can be obtained through mail order catalogues. The reason that I recommend this type of set is that, not only can one obtain the standard BBC shipping forecasts, but also weather and shipping information from coastal radio stations which very often broadcast matters of interest to the small cruiser navigator. Information regarding frequencies and times is to be found in all the nautical almanacs. By whatever means it is obtained, weather information is extremely important to a navigator in making up his mind as to his course of action during the following few hours. If any gale warnings come up for the area in which I am sailing, I scoot for shelter or, if already there, I stay there. Radio information regarding visibility is also of great value in decision making. If the navigator is not the skipper, he must use his experience and knowledge to help the skipper in making decisions, particularly those which affect the safety of the crew and boat.

From the ordinary radio receiver we go on to the transmitter/receiver (transceiver), a set which not only receives messages, but can transmit them to other vessels or to shore. For yachts, these transceivers cover two sets of frequencies: Medium Wave/Radio Telephony (MF/RT) Marine Band, and Very High Frequency Radio Telephony (VHF/RT). The MF/RT sets employ single side-band techniques (SSB) which means that they are expensive, and must be considered beyond the means of most small boat owners, but it must be said that their range (up to two hundred miles) does make them attractive.

At a much lower cost there are the VHF/RT sets, the operation of which, since they are crystal tuned, is simplicity itself and well within the capabilities of the average sailing man, but it must be realised that an operator's licence is required for them. Since these sets operate on very high frequency radio waves their range is more or less limited to line of sight. The absolute maximum range of a VHF set depends upon the quality and height of the aerial and the power output (25 watts max) of the sets. Under optimum conditions it is possible to operate effectively at a range of forty miles. VHF sets can operate in three modes, depending upon how they are equipped. For sets equipped with the Simplex mode only, it is necessary to use standard voice procedure. That is to say that when one person has finished speaking he must say 'Over' and release his transmit switch because his set will not transmit and receive simultaneously. Messages on one VHF channel can only travel one way at a time, like liquid in a pipe where the direction of flow is controlled by a valve. If the liquid is flowing in one direction it cannot accept a flow in the opposite direction at the same time; the valve must be altered to reverse the flow. The transmit switch on a VHF set equipped with the Simplex mode acts like the valve; press it and the message flows from you to the other set. When the transmit switch is released the set can receive an incoming message. It is for this reason that it is sometimes erroneously stated that Simplex-equipped sets cannot be used for link calls (telephone from yacht to telephone number ashore via a coastal radio station). They can be so used, but the person on the telephone ashore *must* obey the correct voice procedure and say 'Over' each time he or she has finished speaking so that the yacht's operator knows when to press his transmit switch and start speaking. For normal ship-to-ship and ship-to-shore (Coastguard or coastal radio station) the Simplex mode is perfectly adequate.

A frequently quoted disadvantage with Simplex is that it gives no privacy; anyone can tune into the channel in use, and listen in on the conversation. As far as I am concerned, I do not in the least mind if this happens when I am making any type of call, but for the business man who uses his VHF radio to keep in touch with his office, this could prove very undesirable. The Semi-Duplex mode does give the privacy advantage but does not give the 'telephone type conversation' that is available with Duplex.

The Duplex mode, although it adds to the cost of the set, does have the advantage of privacy as well as providing 'telephone type' conversation; in other words it obviates the necessity of having to say 'Over' at the end of each period of speech, and both ends of the 'line' can speak at once if they so wish. Considerable discipline is required on the part of the yacht's operator not to keep his transmit switch pressed for longer than is absolutely necessary because transmitting makes a far greater demand on the battery than does receiving. The Duplex system works by using two channels at opposite ends of the marine broadcast spectrum. The ship sends on Channel 'A' and receives on Channel 'B', and the shore station sends on Channel 'B' and receives on Channel 'A'; consequently, in order to listen in on a conversation on Duplex, one would need to know both the channels in use, and to have one receiver for each channel.

There is always argument amongst yachtsman, and I have known the Coastguards to join in, regarding the number of channels needed aboard a yacht. There are six-, twelve-, twenty-four- and fifty-six-channel sets on the market. With current congestion on the VHF frequencies, the six-channel set is really only usable for local cruising since its range is limited. The normal channels with one of these sets are 6 (ship-to-ship), 16 (distress and calling channel), 8 (ship-to-ship) and 67 (Coastguard Yacht Safety). This leaves two channels for the owner to choose from.

One of these, which is of considerable use to yachtsmen is Channel M (157.85MHz) which has been allocated to marinas and yacht clubs. The last one could be another private channel or a public correspondence channel, although this latter would limit ability to communicate with the shore if the traffic on the chosen channel should prove to be particularly busy. Alternatively the remaining channel could be 12 or 14 which are allocated to port operations, but this would limit the number of ports one could contact. The twelve-channel sets must have Channels 6 and 16 as these are obligatory for all VHF sets. The remaining channels could be those mentioned for the six-channel sets plus the missing port operations channel and a selection from the ship-to-ship and ship-to-shore channels. The twenty-four-channel sets would have those channels already mentioned plus a choice, at the owner's discretion, of the remaining available channels. The fifty-six-channel sets would have the full complement of numbered channels plus Channel M and another four private ones. These latter sets, whilst covering the entire VHF Marine Band, do cost more than the smaller sets – obviously the individual must weigh convenience against bank balance when making a choice.

Details of all the marine channels and their uses can be found in the nautical almanacs and other maritime publications. The choice of channels used by the smaller sets with only a limited number available must be governed by the cruising area of the boat, and any authoritative publication on the subject of VHF radio should be carefully consulted before making a choice as to the channels to be fitted to your particular set. Also, it is a sound idea to consult with the local Coastguards because they know the best ones for use in their area.

There is one other type of radio set which the yachtsman must consider – the Callbuoy which is a portable distress radio telephone set which transmits on the International Distress Frequency on medium wave at 2182kHz. The set is completely self-contained and waterproof and can be operated from a yacht, life raft or even by a person in the water. It has a range of between sixty and eighty miles which gives an enormous coverage. For anyone sailing well offshore, whatever the size of boat, a Callbuoy is a must for safety reasons. It can reach other ships or the rescue organisations from a far greater distance than can a VHF set, and it alerts other ships which will either be able to render help themselves, or alert the

Search and Rescue organisations. Its cost is a small premium for the lives of everyone aboard the boat. I have heard it said by people who ought to know better, that a radio transmitter aboard a small boat is an unnecessary luxury. Utter rubbish! A radio transmitter is a small boat's link with the land, a source of confidence at all times, comfort in time of danger and help in time of distress. There is more information about radios in Chapter 5.

There is no worse situation in which a yachtsman can find himself than to get caught in a busy shipping lane by sudden fog. This can happen all round our coasts, and I for one am not ashamed to admit that I am frightened when it happens to me. It even happened once in Plymouth Sound, inside the breakwater. I was beavering away at trying to get the boat over on to the western shore of the Sound to get out of the way of the big chaps, when the Roscoff Ferry loomed out of the fog right on my tail! I knew that she was coming in and could hear her siren; whether she could hear our pipsqueak compressed air horn is doubtful. Fortunately she had a look-out right up in her bows in communication with the bridge, because she altered course surprisingly quickly to starboard. That gives some idea of how fast things can happen in fog, even in inshore waters. One of the navigator's jobs is to

RADAR LOBE

BLIND AREA BENEATH LOBE

Fig 28(i)

RADAR LOBE

RADAR REFLECTOR

Fig 28(ii)

establish, as best he can, the position of other vessels in his area, whether risk of collison exists, and if so what action to take to avoid it. Also he has to keep a running plot going on his chart so that he can, at a moment's notice, say exactly where the yacht is.

It is most unlikely that a mini-cruiser will be equipped with radar, but she must be equipped with the largest and most efficient radar reflector possible, and it must be rigged at the correct attitude and as high as possible. In my opinion the only place for a radar reflector is at the top of the mast, but it must be realised that this will not necessarily produce a 'break' on a big ship's radar screen. There are a number of reasons for this; the most important of which are the attitude of the reflector due to the yacht being heeled, the 'blind' area ahead of the ship, and the amount of 'clutter' on the screen, see Fig 28(i) and (ii). Since at best the 'break' from a yacht's radar reflector will be small and will probably only appear intermittently, there is a strong chance that the officer of the watch will miss the yacht altogether. In other words, she will not be 'seen', especially in rough weather when the reflector will be going up and down and can easily be dipping below the bottom of the radar lobe. However, I do know of a number of cases where big ships have altered course for a yacht because the officer of the watch saw the 'break' on the radar screen and recognised it for what it was.

With the new generation of radar reflectors, such as the Firdell, the chances of being 'seen' are greatly increased. But any handyman can make for himself a better reflector than can normally be bought by making up a gang of three reflectors – one above the other – all in the 'catch rain' attitude, but each one offset by 120° from the one below it as shown in Fig 29. The only tools necessary are a hacksaw, a file or two and access to welding gear.

In addition to radar reflectors, there are radar detectors on the market which are within the pocket of most small boat owners. The Marine Check set marketed by Telesonic Marine Ltd and the Watchman made by Lo-Kata Ltd are two such sets which come to mind.

There are some items without which some navigators say they cannot do; course plotters, for instance. In my opinion these and other navigation devices are luxuries for the mini-cruiser, besides which the less gash gear one has floating about the cockpit aboard boats of this size the better. The need for most of them is negated by the Mark V chart board anyway. However, there is one little device, which I invented, which is of some use in the planning stages of a cruise. This is a tidal vector. All it consists of are three pieces of wood held together at the ends by sliding clips which have a pivoting capability. This device is shown in Fig 30 (i) and (ii), and is simply used to work out a course to be sailed, taking tidal stream and speed into account. By using this aid for different courses and boat speeds it is possible to plan a series of courses to be sailed under a number of different conditions of wind and tide.

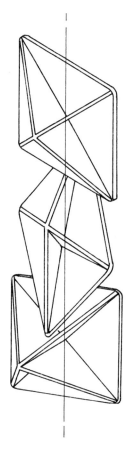

Fig 29

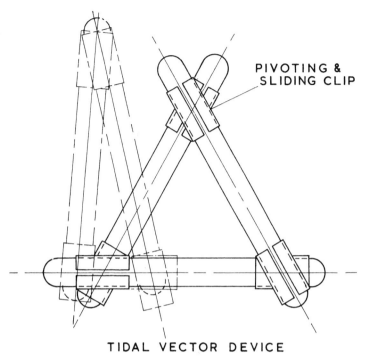

PIVOTING &
SLIDING CLIP

TIDAL VECTOR DEVICE

Fig 30(i)

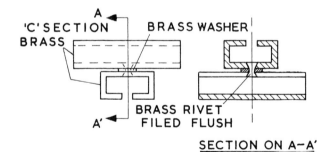

A

'C' SECTION
BRASS

BRASS WASHER

BRASS RIVET
FILED FLUSH

A'

SECTION ON A-A'

Fig 30(ii)

When these have been plotted on to the relevant chart, they can be transferred to a trace which is then put into the cruise planning folder, to be taken out whenever needed for reference. A series of these traces prepared during the winter months, once the next year's tide tables and nautical almanacs are available, will save any navigator an enormous amount of concentrated work as the weeks draw nearer to the date of the cruise. When the actual day of departure dawns, all that has to be done is to take out the relevant trace and transfer all its details on to the passage-making chart. From there on, all one's time can be devoted to actual pilotage and navigation. Only unforeseen circumstances will cause any major alteration in the basic plan. The preparation and use of traces are explained in the next chapter.

Since mini-cruiser long-distance voyages form a very small percentage of the total number of deep-sea voyages, I do not intend to go into the realms of celestial navigation; in any case the subject has been very competently dealt with elsewhere. Nonetheless, although it must be considered a luxury, a sextant is a very useful instrument to have aboard. There are a number of plastic sextants on the market and for small boat purposes they are perfectly adequate. Also, they are considerably cheaper than the normal sextant. It is a popular misconception that the sole use of a sextant is for taking sun and star sights. In fact, with its aid it is possible to obtain a positive fix from objects ashore, as will be explained later.

Aboard small boats it is doubtful if the steering compass is of a type, or in a position, which permits the use of an azimuth ring. This is a device which allows the navigator to take bearings of objects, including the sun, outside the vessel using the steering compass. It consists chiefly of a sighting device coupled to a prism so that an object can be seen through the sights, and its bearing read simultaneously through the prism off the compass card. In order to obtain bearings of important navigational features or other vessels, a hand-bearing compass is, in my opinion, the best instrument for the mini-cruiser navigator. It consists of a small compass with a prismatic sight of one type or another, and a light source so that it can be used at night. The light source may be supplied by torch batteries in the handle with a bulb to illuminate the card, or it can be a Beta light such as in the Mini Compass. It is important to swing the hand-bearing compass so that all bearings taken with it are accurate, and always to use the hand-bearing compass in the position in which it was swung. As with the steering compass, an inaccurate hand-bearing compass is a menace.

In addition to the instruments and aids discussed above, there are a few items which should be part of every cruising boat's inventory. Among these are a barometer, a clock or watch, and

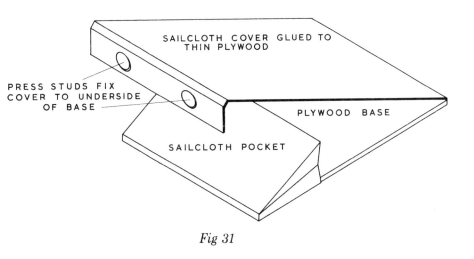

SAILCLOTH COVER GLUED TO THIN PLYWOOD

PRESS STUDS FIX COVER TO UNDERSIDE OF BASE

PLYWOOD BASE

SAILCLOTH POCKET

Fig 31

proper folio covers for charts. The navigator will be as interested as the owner, if the two are not the same person, in the weather, so that a reliable barometer is a must. A conjunction of intelligent reading of the barometer and sound interpretation of weather forecasts can give a reliable guide as to the weather to be expected in one's immediate cruising area. For the safe completion of a passage this is vital. I recommend reading one of the very good books on weather forecasting for yachtsmen which are on the market – they can help a great deal.

An accurate watch or clock is essential for every navigator. I recommend a quartz movement as this gives considerable accuracy with a very even rate. My watch gains two seconds per month, but I would stress that it was expensive. Quite low-priced quartz watches will give a rate of plus or minus a second per week, and this is accurate enough for most purposes.

*Additional Equipment*

Folio covers are essential if charts are to be kept in order and not get misplaced. Using the small A3 size charts which I recommend, it is very easy to misplace one unless they are kept in numerical order in a chart folio, see Fig 31. This habit of keeping charts in their right order is something I learnt very early on.

4
Basic Methods Without Electronic Aids

Everyone who drives a car has at some time or another used a map, and has taken note of the scale. Until recently the most popular maps were the Ordnance Survey one-inch-to-a-mile series, the representative fraction (RF) of which is quoted on the maps as 1:63360. This means that one inch measured on the map represents 63,360 inches $(1760 \times 3 \times 12 = 63,360)$ on the actual ground. This RF is also called the natural scale. The modern metric series of Ordnance Survey maps is to a natural scale of 1:50,000, which means that one metric unit measured on the map represents 50,000 of the same units on the actual ground; thus one metre on the map represents 50,000 metres or 50 kilometres on the ground, and one millimetre on the map represents 50,000 millimetres or 50 metres on the ground. The small figure on the natural scale represents the map and the large figure represents the ground. As with maps, so with charts, but the natural scale of a chart is based on the scale of latitude and distance; since charts are to Mercator's projection this scale will vary between the Equator and the Poles, but for any given latitude the scale of latitude on the left- and right-hand margins of the chart is correct for that latitude, and so one minute $(0° \ 1')$ represents the British Standard Nautical Mile of 6080 feet (1853.18 metres).

Most countries outside Britain use the International Nautical Mile of 6076.06 feet (1852 metres), but British yachtsmen use the British Standard Nautical Mile of 6080 feet which is divided up into 10 cables of 608 feet or 200 yards approximately. Charts are published to a number of natural scales, and all British publications are based on the BSNM which is usually abbreviated to n mile. (It should here be noted that the Statute Mile which is used on land is one of 5280 feet [1609.34 metres] and is not used in navigation at sea.) The natural scales which we, as British yachtsmen, use vary from 1:768,600 at latitude 50°N to river charts at 1:28,062 or 2.6 inches to one nautical mile.

The scale of the chart one uses must depend upon its purpose. For instance, it would not be a very good idea to use a series of charts of 1:100,000 for planning a cruise from Heybridge Basin to the Isles of Scilly. Neither would much good come from trying to navigate across the Thames Estuary using a chart to a scale of 1:500,000 or 1:750,000. For crossing the North Sea a chart to a scale of 1:750,000 to 1:200,000 is amply good enough, and at the western end of the English Channel charts to the same scales would fit the bill admirably. For coastwise passage making I would recommend charts to a scale of 1:75,000 to 1:100,000 for the English Channel, but for the East Coast I would go for a scale which gives more detail of the sandbanks and buoyage system; something in the region of 1:50,000. It must be realised that the smaller the natural scale or RF, the larger the amount of detail, and that for sailing in difficult waters one should employ the smallest natural scale available. Oddly enough, a chart to a scale of 1:50,000 is referred to as a large scale, and one to 500,000 is called a small-scale chart.

On all charts it will be seen that there are one or more compass roses, and that these consist of two concentric rings, both marked off from 0° to 360°, but with an offset on the inner circle of between 4° and 8° West. The North–South axis of the outer ring is parallel to the lines of longitude on the chart, and is the TRUE North–South. The axis of the inner ring, which is a few degrees West of True North, is MAGNETIC North–South, see Fig 1, p13. The amount by which Magnetic North varies from True North is called Magnetic Variation, and is not constant; it changes from year to year. Also, it changes according to geographical position. On the East–West axis of the Magnetic compass rose is shown the amount of Magnetic Variation, the year for which it had that value, and the annual rate of change, but since this is so small and takes between ten and twelve years to change by one degree, it can to all intents and purposes be ignored by the small boat sailor, see Figs 1 and 32. For example, on my current chart of the southern North Sea the Magnetic Variation is shown as being 5°W in 1979, decreasing by about 5' annually (1' is 1/60th of 1°). So, by 1991 it

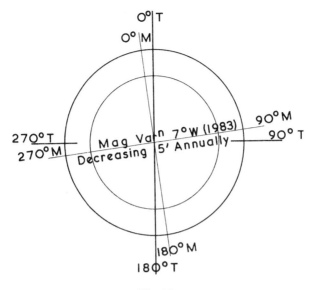

Fig 32

will be 4°W, and 1° is neither here nor there when steering a small boat.

To change from True to Magnetic, one adds the Variation if it is West, and subtracts if it is East. So the first thing a navigator has to do is to check on the amount and direction of Magnetic Variation. But he also has another variant with which to deal. This is Compass Deviation which represents the individual characteristics of a particular compass. Take the compass out of one boat and put it into another, and it will have a different set of characteristics or Deviation. In the chapter on navigation equipment I talked about swinging the compass; this is done to establish the amount of Deviation in a compass at 10° intervals throughout the whole 360°. Because most steel-built boats have an inherent magnetism, the Deviation of the compass can be quite considerable, and in order to reduce it to ensure the accuracy of the compass, the compass adjuster positions correcting magnets in the best place to obtain an overall reduction in the Deviation for that particular compass. When he has completed his work, the compass adjuster supplies the owner with a Deviation Card which gives the amount of Deviation of his compass for each 10° from 0° round to 360°. Each time a navigator works out a course or bearing he has to refer to the Deviation Card so that he can make the necessary adjustments to his calculations. Since, in the Straits of Dover, Magnetic Variation was 7°W in 1979, decreasing by about 5' annually, it will take six years to change by 30', and because many small boat compasses are only graduated in 2° intervals, the navigator can ignore the annual change.

However, he has to take Magnetic Variation into account when plotting a course, and this is how he does it. Let us assume that a yacht is in Dover Harbour, and that the owner/navigator wants to cross the Channel to Calais. Because the Regulations state that a vessel crossing the separation lanes *must do so as near at right angles as is practicable*, this means that he cannot steer a direct course for Calais, but must take a course which will take him across the separation lanes at 90°. From the chart this turns out to be a course of 131° True. He now has to correct this for Magnetic Variation *and* Compass Deviation.

131° True plus Magnetic Variation at 4°W = 135° Magnetic.
Compass Deviation for 140°M is 2° East.
∴ 135°M−2°E = 133° Compass.

This is the still water compass course. Allowance now has to be made for other variants, which include tidal stream, surface drift (if any) and leeway; so let us complete the calculations.

The navigator draws in the compass course of 133°C on the chart to carry him clear of the separation lane on the French side of the Straits. Knowing his boat, he works out what his speed should be under the wind conditions at the time; say, 5 knots. From the entrance of Dover Harbour to clear the separation lanes on the French side is 14 miles which will take him 3 hours at his estimated speed. He adds 1 mile to the actual distance to carry him clear of the north-bound lane. On a piece of paper he draws a line at 133° and scaled (chart scale) 15 miles long. From the tidal atlas and tide tables he obtains the following information:

At the time he plans to leave, the tidal stream is flowing at ½ to 1 knot at 45°T.
One hour after leaving it is flowing at 1 to 1.5 knots at 45°T.
Two hours after it is flowing at 1 to 3 knots at 45°T.
During the third hour the tidal stream is flowing at 1 to 2 knots at 45°T.

He writes down the averages because it is half-way between Springs and Neaps.

Zero hour average rate of stream = 1kn
After 1 hour average rate of stream = 1.25kn
After 2 hours average rate of stream = 1.5kn
3rd hour average rate of stream = 1kn

= 4.75kn

∴ Average tidal stream for 3 hours = 4.75÷4 = 1.875kn

He will be quite safe in allowing for a tidal rate of 1.8kn, and he multiplies this by three (estimated time to clear the lanes) and arrives at a figure of 5.4. This is the amount he will be carried by the tide at 45°T. He now corrects for Magnetic Variation, so adds 4°

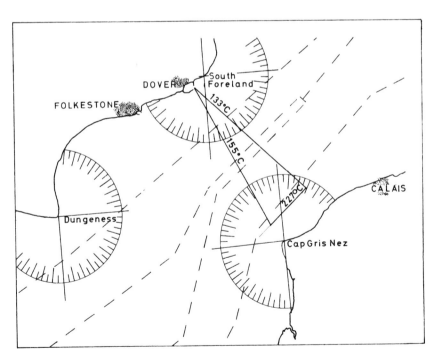

Fig 33

and subtracts 2°E for Compass Deviation. He has now reduced everything to the same value, ie compass degrees. On his piece of paper he draws an angle on the reciprocal of 47°C at the outer end of his 15-mile line, and scales the line at 5.4 n miles. He joins the end of this line to the Dover end of the 15-mile line, and this gives him the course to steer in order to cross the separation lanes at 90° *over the ground*. This proves to be 155° Compass. His working on the chart is shown in Fig 33.

In this particular case surface drift and leeway could be ignored as they would be negligible; had it been blowing hard for more than twenty-four hours, he would probably have to make an allowance for surface drift, but with the wind coming from almost dead abeam he could still afford to ignore leeway. What in fact the navigator did in this case was to draw a tidal vector. Always remember to draw the direction of tidal flow on the reciprocal of the actual direction of tide, and don't forget to make the necessary corrections for Magnetic Variation and Compass Deviation. I have known many navigators to forget these two corrections, with the result that they did not end up at their intended destination. It was only afterwards, when checking their calculations, that I discovered their errors.

To revert to the above example, had the wind been blowing at an angle of less than 60° off the bow, the best thing to have done would have been to cross the separation lanes under power. The calculations for course would have been exactly the same.

To revert to the compass; there are three separate North points – True North which is in the direction of the North Pole, Magnetic North which is in the direction of the North Magnetic Pole, and Compass North which is in the direction taken by the North-seeking pole of the compass needle, and is individual to each compass, see Fig 34 (i) to (iii). Corrections for Magnetic are 'add for West', 'subtract for East'; if one is a purist, it varies from year to year. Corrections for Compass Deviation are the same, but it does not vary from year to year; nonetheless, it is not a bad idea to swing the compass once every five years. In that time there may have been additions to and deletions from the boat's equipment, some of which could be made of ferrous metal and thus affect the compass for better or for worse. Also, should it be found necessary to alter the position of the compass, it should be swung in its new position. Finally, Magnetic Variation remains the same no matter

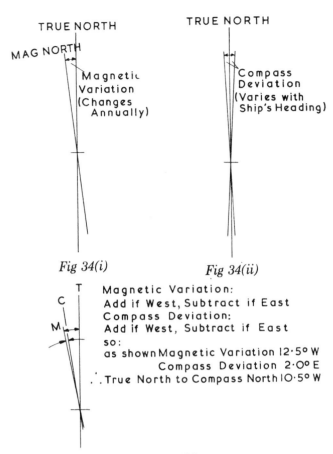

TRUE NORTH

MAG NORTH

Magnetic
Variation
(Changes
Annually)

Fig 34(i)

TRUE NORTH

Compass
Deviation
(Varies with
Ship's Heading)

Fig 34(ii)

T

C

M

Magnetic Variation:
Add if West, Subtract if East
Compass Deviation:
Add if West, Subtract if East
so:
as shown Magnetic Variation 12·5° W
Compass Deviation 2·0° E
∴ True North to Compass North 10·5° W

Fig 34(iii)

what the boat's heading, whereas Compass Deviation changes with the vessel's heading.

Having dealt with the corrections the navigator has to make for the compass, we come to the outside influences for which he has to allow when deciding on the actual course to steer. I have already mentioned them: surface drift and leeway. Unfortunately for the navigator both of these are variables. Surface drift depends upon wind speed and direction, and also for how long the wind has been blowing from that direction. Remember that the direction of wave motion has little or no bearing on surface drift, so do not be led into thinking that it does. Waves do not always travel in exactly the same direction as the wind. The method of estimating the speed and direction of surface drift is simple enough. Stand with your back to the *true* wind and the direction of drift will be 40° to your right front in the Northern Hemisphere (left front in the Southern), and the speed will be 2 per cent of the speed of the true wind.

The amount of leeway depends upon the individual boat, her point of sailing and conditions of wind and sea. Obviously, downwind leeway will be nil, and it will increase as the boat comes round on to the wind. The best way of computing the combined effects of surface drift and leeway is to judge from the first 2 miles or so of sailing from the point of departure. Take a bearing on a feature dead astern and then, when the log reads 2 miles, take another. The difference between the first and second bearings will give the combined angle of leeway and surface drift. With this information, the navigator can draw a drift and leeway vector to add to his Estimated Course. On passage, this should be the last bit of special plotting and calculating that is required until the tide turns, when a fresh set will have to be produced.

Having performed all these tricks, a navigator would be forgiven for thinking that his work was well done, but it is not over. At least once every two hours he has to transfer the deck log information to his notebook and then work out his Estimated Position. This needs to be checked once every four hours either by a fix from visual bearings or by RDF. Should there be a large discrepancy between the EP and the fix, the latter must be taken as being nearer to the boat's actual position, and any course adjustments made. And so he continues through the long and weary night and the next day until port is reached. Being a navigator is no sinecure aboard any boat, but aboard a minicruiser it is a hard, hard slog.

Navigation is a continuing process which starts as early as possible before passage planning begins. It must be assumed that, aboard a small cruiser, the owner is also the navigator. If not then it is up to the owner to let his navigator know his plans as soon as possible. The first action is to obtain small-scale charts of the whole area of the projected cruise, thus enabling the navigator to, as it were, see the whole picture at once. For this purpose, I use small-scale Admiralty Charts, and spend hours just looking at the charts, soaking up as much information as possible. By doing this I build up a large amount of detail in my head, some of which goes into the passage-planning notebook, while the rest – because it does not bear immediate relevance to the route envisaged – remains in my head in case of need. All my planning charts are their original size, and I draw projected courses on them in 2B pencil, modifying as I go along until I reach a point where I am satisfied that I can make no further improvements. This of course includes possible alterations which might need to be made through force of weather or some other circumstance dictating a course of action which differs from the original plan.

One point I do make is to keep open-sea courses as short as possible with a maximum of twelve hours, because sailing a small boat for long periods can be very tiring, especially when one reaches my age! Also, I plan my departure for a time which will bring me towards the coast during the hours of darkness; preferably the last hour or two before dawn. By doing this I can take advantage of the distance at which one can pick up lighthouses in the dark, and so begin the coastwise section having obtained a positive fix on one or more of them.

Another point I make, and one to which I attach considerable importance, is to draw up a list of the nearest harbours along the route to which I can run in the event of unforeseen heavy weather; and on this point, I take Force 6 as the wind strength at which I look for the nearest shelter, and make for it. After all, I cruise for pleasure and can find nothing good to be said for masochism! Any wind force up to 6 is acceptable but at the top end of that force the fun has gone out of things, and one is left with a struggle for survival which is never pleasant. The problems attendant upon plotting a course to the chosen shelter in heavy weather are reduced by knowing beforehand where it is. At the planning stage I also make a list of all the lighthouses and navigation marks which will be met with along the way, together with notes regarding any hazards which might present me with problems.

When I have completed all this preliminary planning, I get down to the fine detail, and start by dividing the route into sections of one day's sail of not more than ten hours at a stretch. This allows two hours for mistakes or changes in the weather. In order to calculate distances to be covered each day, I assume a wind strength of Force 3 to 4 and a direction between due South and North-West. Should the wind go bad on me by coming right on the nose, I have immediate resort to the engine in order to make my destination before nightfall. The same applies if the wind falls light. I must say that I only use the engine as a last resort; I loathe the thing. But sometimes it has to be used, so part of my planning involves making sure that I have sufficient petrol for the maximum distance to be covered plus at least 25 per cent for emergencies. There is nothing more embarrassing and infuriating than to run out of fuel just outside a harbour entrance; and it can also be dangerous. Always allow for the unforeseen and you reduce the risks considerably. It is at the planning stage that these occurrences *must* be anticipated and allowed for. I call these the 'K' factors, and where they can occur I add 25 per cent to allow for them. I remember my father, from whom I learnt a great deal about navigation, saying that the good navigator made an allowance for every contingency that might arise, and then added a little bit more, and that to be a good navigator one had to be something of a pessimist so that everything that came out in your favour was a bonus.

Having completed all his planned courses and lists, the navigator transfers everything to his passage-making charts and his navigation notebook. But before he does this, he will be wise to make A3 size traces on polyester film of the entire planned route including as much detail as is necessary for him to recognise the meaning of the trace. All the charts shown in this book are reproductions of traces. To make a trace, fix the chart firmly to a drawing board or smooth table. Using a mild-strength draughting tape, fix an A3 size sheet of polyester tracing film over the portion of the chart to be traced. Trace in the coastal outlines and any features (outlying rocks etc) which have an important place in the overall plan. Don't forget to add in lines of latitude and longitude and the scale of miles taken from the left- or right-hand margins of the chart. Tracing can be done with a fine-point felt-tipped pen. With regard to colours, I always use black for the coastlines and red or green for the planned courses, but a key must be shown on the trace to indicate the meanings of the colours employed. The same process can be carried out for making a trace of an actual course sailed. One important fact: lines drawn with a felt-tipped pen are water washable, so don't let the traces get wet. As an experienced draughtsman, I prefer to use waterproof drawing inks and special pens for my traces.

The traces completed, the navigator goes back to his small-scale charts and begins to transfer the courses on to his A3 size passage-making charts in black Chinagraph pencil. Proposed four-hourly positions can be marked as shown in Fig 35. If this position is in sight of land, a lightship or Lanby, the bearing and distance to it should be indicated as shown in Fig 36. By using the magnetic compass rose and correcting for Deviation, the navigator can enter all his courses in degrees Compass, thereby saving himself time at a later date.

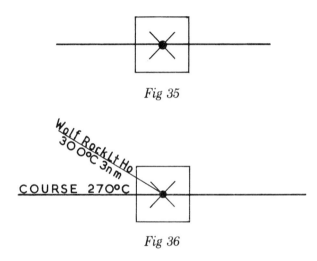

Fig 35

Fig 36

Since there are a number of imponderables in navigation, it is no bad idea to plan courses for the same route but with different wind directions, and here a good deal depends upon experience of an individual boat's capabilities. For instance, it is generally assumed that a boat can sail as close as to within 45° to the true wind. Maybe this is so, but she will not hold to this all the time; the wind does not blow continually from exactly the same direction, added to which the boat will point higher in the puffs than in the lulls. Only experience of the boat will tell the navigator what she will average to windward while making her best speed for a particular wind strength. Different boats are affected more or less by the action of waves. In planning it is necessary to take all these factors into account to assess the likely performance under average conditions, if such things exist. For my boat I never allow for a closer-winded ability than 50° to the true wind. In a Force 4 wind she only appears to make about 2° leeway and her sea-kindliness is such that in a seaway in the English Channel she appears not to be affected by wave action. However, in the short steep seas of the Thames Estuary I would allow another degree or two for wave effect. Were I making for Morlaix from Salcombe I would lay off a direct line course of 192°M, distance 88 n miles. With a wind South of South-West I could not lay the rhumb line (direct course), and would have to tack. The question which would then arise would be which would be the favoured tack? See Fig 37(i), where Wind 1 relates to Angle 1 and so on. In each case it is best to choose the worst condition which could prevail, assuming a wind speed of 17 knots. This would be from the West-South-West to South-South-East. Since sailing under these conditions would involve at least twenty-four hours at sea (the first leg of a cruise can always last this long if there are at least two helmsmen), one can ignore the effect of the tides since they will cancel out, and the

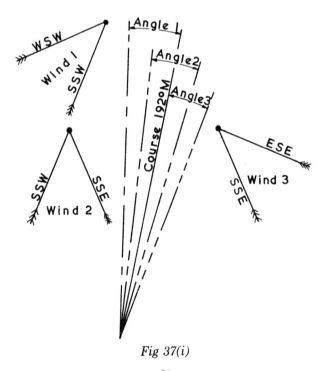

Fig 37(i)

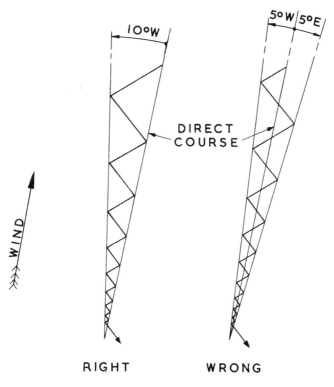

Fig 37(ii)

rhumb line would be from Bolt Head to Stolvezen Buoy at the entrance to Morlaix River.

Now the choice has to be made whether to set the angle of approach to windward of the rhumb line, to leeward of it, or right down the middle. With the wind from West-South-West there is no choice but to sail a mean course of 10°W of the rhumb line to the rhumb line itself. If the wind veers to South-West by South as shown in Fig 37 (ii) the 10°W angle would be about 3 miles to the good after six tacks, so it would be about 4 to 5 miles to the good by the time the apex of the angle was reached. The 5° either side of the course would finish up evens, whilst the 10°E angle would end up about 3½ to 4 miles to the bad; in other words it would mean at least another hour at sea. If the wind backed to South-South-East all three angles of approach would benefit considerably. If it only went back as far as South, the two outer angles in Fig 38 would be

81

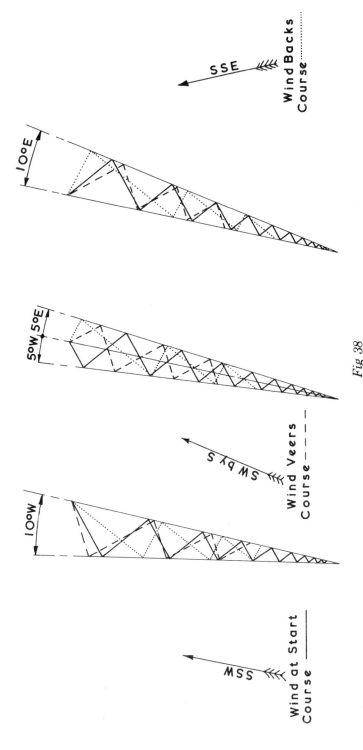

Fig 38

the losers, and the middle one would gain slightly. This example shows how valuable planning on the latest weather forecast can be. Never sail so that the mean course drops to leeward of the chosen one. Should the wind be blowing from East-South-East, then the angle of approach could be 5° either side of the rhumb line, see Fig 38. In either case, should the wind veer you will have gained considerably; should it back, you will not have lost too much.

These cases show the importance of forward and intelligent planning, choosing the plan best suited to the weather conditions when you set out and, providing that there is no major change in the weather, *sticking to it*. Do not alter a plan half-way through the trip unless there is a very sound reason indeed for doing so; that way lies uncertainty and despondency later on. I remember leaving Plymouth bound for Treguier on the North Brittany coast. With the wind West of South-West we could lay the entrance to Treguier River easily without having to strap everything in hard, and we had a very comfortable ride until, for no known reason, the navigator (not me!) decided to alter course for the Sept Iles Lighthouse which we picked up shortly before dawn. Instead of altering back to the mouth of Treguier River, he stood on until we were almost up to the Sept Iles themselves. In the meantime the wind backed, and we finished up with a most uncomfortable slog, short tacking in a very lumpy sea along that horribly rock-strewn coast. Had the navigator stuck to his original plot, the amount of windward work would have been reduced to, according to my later calculations, one short leg to get us to windward of the river mouth, followed by a long leg into and up the river.

The angle of approach may worry some people, but there is nothing to it. It is simply an angle between the arms of which all tacks are confined, the optimum angle being 10°. Any angle greater than this and too much sea is being covered for the ground gained, while the chances of making an accurate land-fall are reduced. Any angle less than 10° means too many tacks for the ground covered, see Fig 39 (i) and (ii). Apart from anything else, this can be tiring for the crew, upsetting (literally) for the cook, and generally bad for morale.

In addition to planning courses for a cruise, since the navigator also has to get the boat safely into harbour, he not only has to plan the pilotage into the ports and harbours it is intended to visit, but

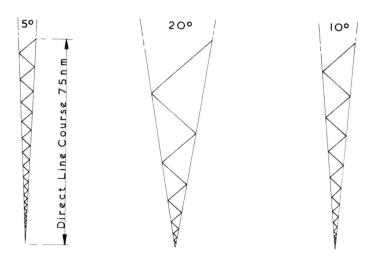

Fig 39(i)

Angle	Area Covered	Course Run	Tacks	% Distance	% Tacks
5°	236sq m	103n m	34	Nil	Plus 161·5
10°	483sq m	106n m	21	Plus 3	" 61·0
20°	966sq m	113n m	13	" 10	Nil

Fig 39(ii)

also into those to which it might be necessary to make for shelter. In his navigation notebook he should enter the name of each place together with the number of the relevant page in whichever pilot's guide he uses. For instance, he might be cruising down West to the Isles of Scilly and would enter the appropriate page numbers from the *South of England Pilot* or the *Macmillan Silk Cut Nautical Almanac*, as well as the number of the relevant large-scale chart in the folio which gives details of the entrance, anchorages and moorings. It is no use planning a cruise and at the last minute, possibly in the dark, searching through one or more books to find the way into a harbour, especially if it has started to blow up a bit. Far better to know exactly where to look for the information you need and to be able to get at it quickly. I find that if I have the time to read up the details of an entrance, I can absorb a major part of that information and, as a result, the nagging worries that can beset a navigator when approaching an unknown harbour are greatly reduced. I have spoken to people who have got themselves into trouble while trying to make entrance to a strange harbour who have either said 'I couldn't find it in the pilot's guide' or 'I couldn't make the channel out'. In other words they had not done their homework properly. Never try to make an unknown entrance blind; good advance planning will tell you where to find quickly the details you want; this is a small premium to pay to ensure safe arrival.

In the navigator's notebook therefore there will be entries referring to the planned course traces, the passage-making chart numbers, details of entrances to harbours and estuaries, and any special hazards or possible problem areas for which to keep a look-out. This notebook needs to be fairly large because it will contain more than the planning notes; it will contain information about each day's sailing (written up the day before), as well as the navigation log and space for calculations. The good navigator takes with him a plentiful supply of tracing material, pencils (HB and 2B), more than one pencil eraser and, if he uses the encapsulated charts described in Chapter 1, a large supply of Chinagraph pencils (black, green, red and yellow), and a block of notepaper for making additional notes and performing all the odds and ends of calculation that make up so much of a navigator's life.

I use the second half of my navigation notebook as the navigation log. I write details of courses, times and extracts from the deck log, plus any other relevant information such as times of high and low water, and the log reading at the time of departure. This latter is vital because no one will remember the reading an hour later, let alone three or four hours on. If for any reason I have to take a sun sight, which is very infrequent in my sailing area, I use a sheet of the type recommended by Mary Blewitt in her book *Celestial Navigation for Yachtsmen*. When completed, it is put into the boat's log. By keeping this separated from the navigation notebook I eliminate the possibilities of muddling up two entirely different types of working. I would add here that, so as to keep his papers, charts, notebooks, etc in order, the navigator should have some type of waterproof satchel or hold-all. This must be of a size to hold at least three A3 size chart folios, tidal atlas, nautical almanac, notepad, sheets of tracing film, all his instruments (in a separate pocket), and it is no bad thing to include pads of weather forecast sheets and the ship's log, either in the form published by a number of firms, or a good A4 size stiff-backed notebook ruled up to suit the method of entry. The radio log, if a radio transceiver is carried, should also be a stiff-backed notebook ruled up to suit and be kept in a safe place near the radio set. The main ship's log will carry a certain amount of information transferred from the navigation log such as the EPs as they are worked up, and any positive fixes obtained.

Lastly, on the subject of mini-cruise planning, I would stress the fact that this can make or mar a cruise, so it must be as thorough and accurate as possible and, once the whole cruise is planned, re-written in the correct sequence.

I have talked about planning in relation to cruising, but in these days of trailer-sailers when the point of departure can be a different place each week-end, it is sound policy to plan the week-end cruise on week-day evenings, especially if the area is unknown. A few hours spent in encapsulating new charts, looking at them and making relevant notes, will be amply repaid by a couple of days free from worry about safe navigation.

When making a coastwise passage of a few hours' duration, three things need to be taken into consideration: the best course or courses for reaching the destination, obstacles to these, and the weather in all its aspects. Let us assume that the first leg of an intended cruise is to be from Burnham-on-Crouch to Lowestoft, and that it has been decided to leave Burnham just before high water at 0350hrs. The weather forecast has given a wind from the South-West, Force 4 with a bright sunny day. At 0330hrs you are under way with the first of the ebb under you after the first half hour, and you make the Whittaker Beacon at 0500hrs. The trace (Fig 40) shows that the best course takes you within $3\frac{1}{2}$ miles of Orfordness at 41 n miles. The only likely obstacle on this course is the Gunfleet sand, and it takes you just under a mile along its Eastern side. Having deducted the necessary 2° for Compass Deviation from the Magnetic course of 61°, you give the helmsman a course of 59° Compass to the sunk light vessel 21 miles distant. For the first three hours you will have $1\frac{3}{4}$ knots of tide under you, so that you will reach the light vessel after

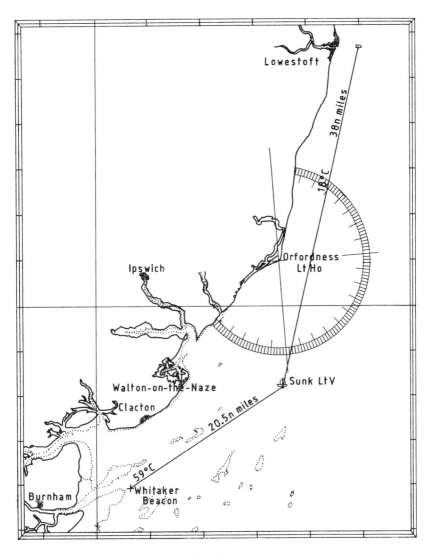

Fig 40

approximately two hours and forty minutes, and for the next two hours you will still have one knot to help you on your way. You will however have to alter course at the light vessel for the West Newcombe Buoy 38 miles distant. This means that you can add just over 7 miles to your distance run after five hours. With a Force 4 South-Westerly and a spinnaker set, you should make a good 6 knots. So, with 1·4 knot tide under you, you'll be making 7.4 knots over the ground with no leeway to allow for. Surface drift will be negligible, but it is as well to check by taking a bearing on the Whittaker Beacon just after altering course, and another after 2 miles have been registered on the log. This will show the combined effect of tide and drift. But under the circumstances I

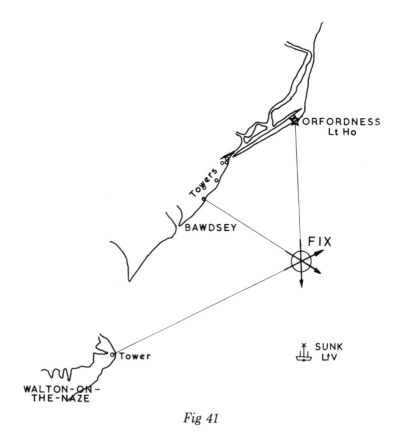

Fig 41

have outlined, it is my guess that these effects will have no appreciable influence on the course to be steered.

As the boat sails up the coast there will be a number of features on which the navigator will be able to obtain a fix. The first two are Clacton Pier and the Tower on Walton Naze. In the chapter on charts I describe how compass roses are drawn round important navigational features. On my East Coast chart I have drawn a rose round Orfordness lighthouse. The method of using this is as follows. Standing in the best position for using the mini compass, take a bearing on Walton Tower, and if you can see it – and with good visibility you should – repeat for the southernmost of the Bawdsey radar towers, and the Sunk light vessel. In each case

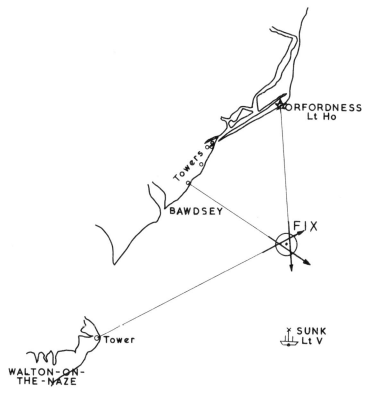

Fig 42

where the bearings are greater than 180°, it will be necessary, in order to obtain back bearings from them, to subtract that sum from the bearing obtained. Where the bearing is less than 180°, it is necessary to add that amount. Then, using the centre point of the compass rose, the straight edge of the pantograph is locked on to a bearing, and a straight line drawn from the relevant point. This is repeated for each feature in turn. There will then be three lines drawn on the chart, and where they cross will be the boat's position as shown in Fig 41. The time interval between the bearings, if short, can be ignored. Should there be an appreciable time interval, the result of drawing in the back-bearing lines will be a triangle or 'cocked hat' as in Fig 42. In fact, the chances are that not even a set of simultaneous bearings would produce a one-point crossing of the back-bearing lines, but the centre of the triangle will be the boat's position as near as makes no odds. If the triangle is a large one the navigator will, having checked his work, take a fresh round of angles, this time taking more care.

As the passage proceeds, Orfordness will come in sight and this can now be used for fixes. Each time a fix is obtained, the navigator plots it on the chart and compares it with his planned course. In between obtaining fixes the navigator should keep a running plot going, using courses steered and readings from the log. This produces the Estimated Course (EC), and each time it is worked up the result gives the Estimated Position (EP). The difference between the EC and the course obtained from fixes should not, on such a passage as this, be very much. But where there is an appreciable difference the course obtained from fixes is the one to rely on. In the event of the course sailed differing from that which was planned, the navigator has to work out the alteration necessary to come back on to it.

When Orfordness lighthouse is abeam, by taking a running fix on it it is possible to obtain a positive point of departure, or by doubling the angle on the bow. To obtain a running fix, a bearing is taken of a fixed object – in this case the lighthouse – and at the same time the log is read. After sailing *on the same course* for a period of time which gives a reasonably open angle, another bearing is taken and the log is read again. By drawing the two back bearings on the chart the two main lines for the method are in place. The first log reading is subtracted from the second, and the distance run is the result. This distance is marked off, to chart

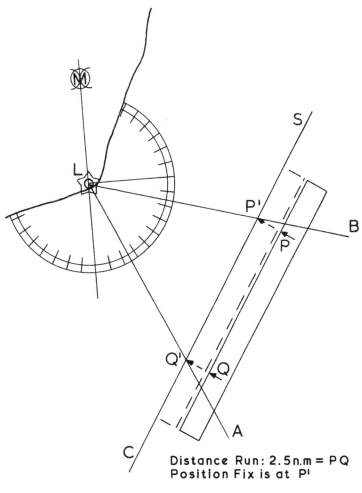

Distance Run: 2.5n.m = PQ
Position Fix is at P¹

Fig 43

scale, on a piece of paper which is laid on the chart along the line of
the course sailed, and moved back and forth across the chart until
the two marks on the paper coincide with the back-bearing lines.
The second position is the fix. See Fig 43 where the lines LA and
LB are the two back-bearing lines. PQ is the scaled edge of the
piece of paper, CS is the course steered and P1 and Q1 are the two
points where the distance run coincides with the back-bearing
lines. Remember that PQ must always be parallel to the line CS.

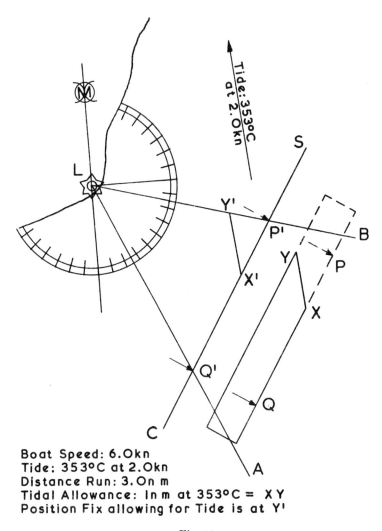

Boat Speed: 6.0kn
Tide: 353°C at 2.0kn
Distance Run: 3.0n m
Tidal Allowance: In m at 353°C = X Y
Position Fix allowing for Tide is at Y'

Fig 44

Using the Mark V chart board one can mark the distance run on
the straight edge in Chinagraph pencil, set the straight edge on
the course steered and move it across until the two points coincide
with the back-bearing lines. When taking a running fix it is often
necessary to make an allowance for the tide, and this is done as
follows. The distance run PQ in Fig 44 is marked off on a strip of
paper and the allowance for tide XY is drawn to scale at the angle

of the tide. The paper is cut or folded along the line XY, and is moved across the chart keeping PQ parallel to CS until PQ corresponds with P'Q'. X'Y' being the tidal allowance, your actual fix will be at Y'.

Doubling the angle on the bow is really only another form of running fix, and can be done in two ways. In method one, the navigator takes the log reading when the object bears 45° on the bow, angle LPQ in Fig 45. The log is again read when the object is abeam at 90°, angle LQP. The distance run between the two log

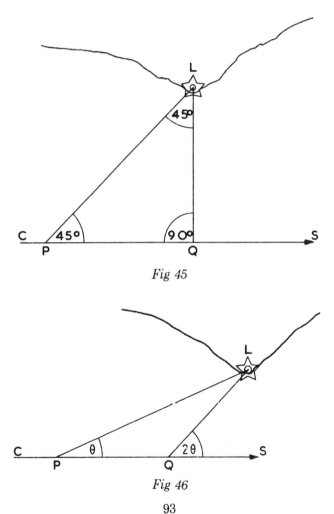

Fig 45

Fig 46

readings is the same as the distance between the object and boat when the former is abeam since the two distances form the equal sides of an isosceles triangle (LQ=LP). In method two a bearing θ, angle LPQ in Fig 46, is taken at the same time as the log is read. When the angle to the object is 2×θ, angle LQS in the same Fig, the log is again read. As in method one, the distance from the object is the same as the distance run, and for the same reason. There are therefore three different ways of obtaining a fix when coastwise cruising. All three are reasonably accurate providing that care is taken when obtaining the bearings. Of the three, I prefer the running fix as it takes less time than obtaining a set of cross bearings, and only requires one point ashore. Using my Mark V chart board the whole thing is very easily worked out. All three methods are considerably simplified if compass roses are drawn as described in Chapter 1.

To return to the trip from Burnham to Lowestoft; the navigator has fixed his position off Orfordness, and has altered course to 020° Compass. From here to Lowestoft he has plenty of features ashore on which to obtain fixes. Among these are three churches, the Signal Station Tower at Southwold, and – if it is getting dark – the light on the North Mole of Lowestoft Harbour. Although he now has to buck a South-going tide, he has brought the yacht safely to where he would have her be. His only remaining problem

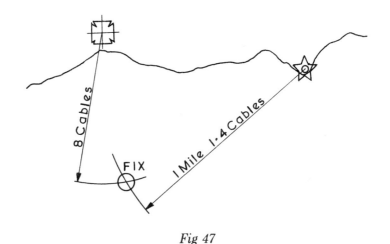

Fig 47

is to get her into the harbour. Since the tide off the harbour entrance runs pretty fast he has to make allowance for this when going in. This is where the pilot's guide and tidal atlas will be of great help.

I want to mention two other methods of obtaining a position fix when coastwise cruising, both of which are accurate and easy to do. The first involves the use of a rangefinder which is a useful instrument to have aboard – not difficult to obtain, but a bit on the expensive side. For this method the compass is not needed at all. One simply obtains the range of two objects which are recognisable on the chart. With each object as centre, the ranges as radii, two arcs are drawn as in Fig 47. The point at which the arcs intersect is the boat's position. There is however one slight snag; some rangefinders are only calibrated in cables up to $1\frac{1}{2}$ miles so they can only be used if one is sailing fairly close inshore, and with a fairly large-scale chart on which to work. One very useful purpose rangefinders do serve is when dodging super tankers and large container ships. The navigator keeps an eye on the compass bearing of the ship, and when she seems to be about a mile away reads off the distance. If the distance then decreases rapidly while the compass bearing alters only very slowly, it is time you weren't there! Always remember that these big boys answer their helms very slowly, take a long time to slow down, and probably haven't seen you anyway. This, in my opinion, applies to all merchant ships, and I always alter course so as to pass at least one cable astern of them. The Royal Navy are very good indeed – they have probably spotted you before you see them. Nevertheless, I make a very positive alteration of course to show them what my intentions are.

There are lightships, Lanbys and various types of buoy which, providing that they can be recognised on the chart, can be used for obtaining a fix. The chart needs to be fairly large scale so that channel buoys and the like are shown. On the smaller-scale charts only the major buoys are shown, and this could cause confusion. There are plenty of navigation buoys on the East Coast but on the South Coast, where they are fewer and farther between, one has to use shoreline features practically all the way or, as on passage from Plymouth to the Isles of Scilly, one has to go right offshore and sail from the Eddystone lighthouse to the Wolf Rock lighthouse. One does get a sight of one or two headlands, and if they can be recognised, it is possible to get a running fix, but sharp eyesight is needed.

When the passage has been completed, it is a good idea to make a full tracing of planned course, dead reckoning course and actual course sailed as obtained from fixes. In the past I have used these traces to prove to the authorities that I had been where I said I'd been. Also, it is best to transfer all navigation information to the ship's log, and all in correct sequence. When arriving at the port or harbour of destination, write up the yacht's log to date and then present it to the Harbour Master for his signature and stamp.

Having dealt with coastwise passage making, it would seem logical to take a look at crossing the North Sea or the English Channel. The navigator has to plan his courses in the same way as for coastal cruising, but there is one difference; he may have to make for a point at sea, out of sight of land, where there is no mark of any kind. It is possible to choose a point, perhaps 20 miles offshore, where two lighthouses appear over the horizon at the same time. At night this presents few problems, but by day one needs sharp eyesight and good binoculars.

Let us assume that a cruise is planned to cover the Brittany coast from Morlaix westwards. The navigator gets out his planning charts, and having perused them for several hours he makes his decision. There are two lighthouses with long-range lights: the Ile de Batz, Gp Fl (4) 25 sec, 23 miles, and Les Sept Iles, Gp Fl (3) 15sec, 24 miles. This means that one light will come over the horizon when it is 24 miles away, and the other when it is 23 miles away. The navigator chooses these two lights for a number of reasons; firstly, he has planned to be about 20 miles off the coast about two hours before daybreak so that the looms of the lights and the lights themselves will be clearly visible in the dark. The second reason is because the characteristics of the lights are sufficiently different to prevent any confusion in their recognition. Thirdly, he has decided to make his point of approach to the coast from an easily identifiable point. This point is the intersection of the radii of maximum range of visibility of the two lights. But these two radii are not 23 and 24 miles respectively as shown on charts. To these must be added the distance of the horizon from the height of eye of the observer. The height of my eyes when I am sitting down is 2ft 8in. The height of my boat's cockpit above the water line is 18in. So, my height of eye above sea level is 4ft 2in which, according to the tables, gives a horizon distance of $2\frac{1}{2}$ miles. Therefore the ranges of the two lights go up to $25\frac{1}{2}$ miles and $26\frac{1}{2}$ miles respectively.

If the navigator is using the encapsulated charts described in Chapter 1, he will already have drawn the radii of maximum range round each of the lighthouses, and he will have made a note of the geographical position of this point. In this case it works out as 49°10′N, 3°59′W. Upon examination of this point on the chart it will be found that it is exactly on the line joining the western end of Plymouth breakwater and Stolvezen Buoy or the Pot de Feu, the point of safe entry into Morlaix River: the ideal point of approach to the coast. The bearing of the entrance to Morlaix River from Plymouth is 181°M. With the prevailing winds varying between North-West and South-West, the only ones to present any navigation problems are the South-Westerlies. So, the navigator decides to kill the dragon at the earliest opportunity. He therefore draws a 10° line to the West of the rhumb line and then draws a line at 270°M to clear Rame Head by about 1 mile. His Compass Deviation Card shows 2° West deviation for a bearing of 270°, so his first course will be noted as 272° Compass 16 miles. This brings him roughly off the mouth of Fowey River but a mile offshore. Depending on the time of start, he makes due allowance for tidal effect and orders his course accordingly. When the boat reaches a point 1 mile South of Pencarrow Head, he puts the boat about and orders a course of 169° Compass. This will take him on to the intersection point of two lighthouses 60 miles distant.

On this point of sailing he is well up to windward of the rhumb line and sailing fairly free. If the wind backs, which in our part of the world is unlikely, he is in a good position with something in hand before he has to think about taking another tack. In a Force 4 he'll probably be making the best part of 5 knots, so that at the end of 60 miles' sailing the tides will have cancelled out. Remember that they do not always do this, and that allowance has to be made for them if necessary. If everything goes according to plan, and he gets his point of intersection, the navigator alters course on to 182° Compass and, if he can hold that without tacking, after 6 miles he will pick up the light of La Phare de la Lande, Fl 5sec, 23 miles. If he holds this course it will take him safely into the mouth of the river.

What happens, you ask, if he does not hit his point of

intersection, or if there is only one lighthouse on that sector of coast? The answer to the first part of the question is that he takes a bearing on the first light to come over the horizon, converts it to a back bearing and lays it off on the chart. With a bearing and range on the light, he has a fix, see Fig 48; in this drawing I have omitted the compass roses for the sake of clarity, and have only shown the

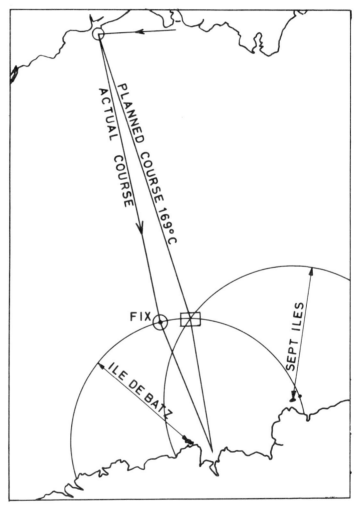

Fig 48

arcs of maximum range of visibility. He now knows where he is, and can plan accordingly. The answer to the second question is the same; he takes a bearing on the light, converts it into a back bearing and lays it off. The point at which the back-bearing line cuts the arc is his position. All this conversion to back bearings and laying off on the chart shows how the drawing of compass roses round all major features and lights pays off in time saved.

The reason I chose the passage from Plymouth to Morlaix is because it just so happens that the point of intersection is exactly on the safe course into Morlaix River. It must be realised that lighthouse characteristics may change and should be checked annually. I bring out this point here because it helps to illustrate the importance of one of the navigator's jobs: that of keeping all his charts up to date through the Admiralty Notices to Mariners. These apply not only to lights, but to the positions of all types of navigation marks and their characteristics, radio beacons and all other navigation information contained on charts which can be subject to alteration. Even soundings can alter. It is not necessary to take the weekly copies of Notices to Mariners – the Hydrographic Department publish special small craft editions, while the *Practical Boat Owner*, amongst other publications, publishes a list of those alterations which are likely to affect yachts, or are of interest to yachtsmen generally. The French charts published by Éditions Cartographiques Maritimes are also subject to alterations, and lists of these can be obtained from the publishers for the cost of the postage from France to the UK.

The principles of navigation remain the same whether it be day or night, but the methods differ. In daylight, providing that visibility remains good, one has the advantage of being able to see unlit marks such as the Whittaker Beacon near the mouth of the River Crouch. This, whilst it requires good eyesight and binoculars, means that keeping on track is simplified. Also, one can see where water shoals or whether there are rocks close to the surface. Consequently it is possible to cut a corner here and there if conditions allow, and to sail much closer to a sandbank than would be prudent at night, especially if one is having to beat to windward along a channel between two banks. By day it is possible to obtain fixes from many different types of topographical feature, and buoys whose positions are shown on the chart. In strong weather when visibility is badly reduced by rain or blown spume, whether it be lit or unlit the next mark ahead can be very hard to find. In a narrow channel when one wants to be able to see the next mark and the one astern, things can be very trying. It is then that good course plotting pays off, and the navigator earns his corn. Taken all in all, daylight passage making, coastwise or offshore, is easier than at night. In the dark one only has lighted marks to go by, and in tricky waters such as the Thames Estuary or the Wash, the navigator *must* know, at any given moment, where he is to within a cable. If not, the boat can be ashore before he knows what has happened. It is for this reason that, until a navigator has gained experience, I always recommend daylight passages coastwise. Until that experience has been gained, one should think very carefully indeed before undertaking a night passage, and under no circumstances whatever try it if the weather forecast is bad. There is no sense in saying 'I've got to be back in the office on Monday without fail' if you are not going to live to see that Monday morning because the boat got into serious trouble through heavy weather, or you ran ashore on to rocks because you did not know exactly where you were. It is not much good relying on the philosophy 'it can't happen to me'. It happens round our coasts all too often every year.

Night navigation calls for care and precision. One must pinpoint every light by its characteristics, and make certain of each and every fix. The skilful use of compass, chart, lead line and watch is very elegant navigation, and a joy to watch. It is also sound practice not to try a tricky passage for the first time at night; one can get into enough bother in daylight, so why add to your difficulties! Night navigation involves using every lighted mark available, getting a bearing on it and if necessary taking a running fix from it. If two or more lights are visible then one can get cross bearings and so obtain a fix that way. Coastwise navigation at night is made fairly easy by lighthouses and lightships. There are not many areas round the coasts of these islands when one cannot see the loom of at least one or the other, and even this can give some idea of the boat's position. Also, don't forget the light cast into the night sky by towns; even such a tenuous source can help to establish a fairly accurate position.

I hate fog and so, I think, do all sailing men and women. As with night navigation, so with fog. Care and precision, and because fog can come down by day or night without warning this is one very good reason for keeping an accurate plot going on the chart at all times. Again, a reliable and accurate watch earns its cost in just one thick fog. Unless the boat is equipped with RDF, and in this chapter we are assuming that she is not, the only instruments of any value are a good log, an accurate compass and a reliable watch. Hold a course for a stated time, check the distance run on the log, change course and repeat. This is where using a lead line in conjunction with a large-scale chart pays off. Keep sailing timed courses, use the lead line and keep the plot going on the large-scale chart, and you will arrive safely at your destination, or the fog will clear so that you can establish your exact position.

If you find yourself in a shipping lane in fog, GET OUT OF IT AS QUICKLY AS POSSIBLE. One of the busiest areas is the mouth of the River Thames, which is also an area very prone to fog. When I used to sail in that area, if fog came down suddenly I would plot a course to the nearest buoy marking the channel. Sailing by lead line and compass, I would stand on until I found the buoy, or until the lead line told me that I was out of the channel. The lead line, in default of an echo sounder, is an essential aboard any boat and can frequently be used to help the navigator if he has lost his way, or is overtaken by darkness or fog. When I was quite sure that I was out of the deep water channel and therefore safe from being run down, I would sail along parallel to the edge of the channel, but well outside the line of the channel buoys, using the lead line all the time. One can sail from buoy to buoy, and it is surprising how, with practice, one can go buoy jumping in fog and meet each one as it is due to come up. If I have to cross a busy channel, I find the narrowest convenient part and then dash across at right angles, using the engine if necessary, although this tends to blank out any noise made by other shipping.

Fog has a nasty habit of disorientating people and of disguising the direction from which a ship is approaching. However, there is a method of getting an approximate idea of the direction of a ship's approach with the aid of a pencil. A boat's hull acts as a sounding box and if you press one end of a pencil against this, and press your ear hard against its other end, you will hear the propeller – and often the engine beats. The ship is coming from the direction where the sound is loudest. This method is sometimes successful in finding a buoy – the sound of water swirling past it can be picked up.

When navigating in fog there is one essential to be borne in mind: the compass, the most important instrument aboard, *must* be trusted. If it serves well in clear weather, it will serve just as well in fog. I have known experienced yachtsmen suspect the accuracy of a perfectly good compass in thick weather, such is the disorientating effect of loss of visibility. The same can apply to the navigation watch; it becomes suspect if a buoy fails to come up on time. In fog, without electronic navigation aids, the navigator must put his trust in those items of equipment which he has at his disposal and which have proved their reliability. Failure to do so can end in disaster. As I have already said, I hate fog, and I dread its coming down when I am in unknown waters, or those which have a mass of dangers, such as the Chenal du Four. But years of experience have taught me to keep my head, use my ears and trust my instruments. Hearing can be a great help, especially when it is used in conjunction with other aids. It is sound practice to have a reliable hand right up forward just listening and reporting anything he hears. I have found that youngsters between the ages of thirteen and sixteen are reliable for this job. They have not learnt to imagine dangers which may or may not exist, and so give fairly accurate reports. Above all, as skipper/navigator never let the crew know that you are worried or frightened, as you may well be; nothing spreads faster than fear, and imagination begins to play tricks on all and sundry.

Approaching an unknown coast can be a worrying time for a navigator. There is, as a result, a tendency to see what one wants or hopes to see, with the not infrequent result that, without warning, the realisation dawns that features are not what they were thought to be, and that one is lost. A way to prevent this is to decide on a particular offshore mark as the landfall point, *and find it* — its name will be painted on it. For instance, there is a port hand, International Association of Lighthouse Authorities (IALA), lateral system buoy at the entrance to Morlaix River called Stolvezen. Coming to the North Brittany coast in daylight, this buoy or the Pot de Feu nearby makes a very good aiming point. Alternatively, approaching the port of Ijmuiden in Holland there is a red and white landfall mark with a red spherical top mark, which is about 5 miles west of the harbour entrance. I always try, if I am to approach a coast in daylight, to make for a very positive landfall mark of this type, and this is a further reason for keeping an accurate plot going. It is dangerous to have a slipshod attitude to navigation at any time, but out of sight of land, when one relies on picking up an actual mark at sea – which may be difficult enough to find in any case according to the conditions – it is nothing short of foolhardy.

As has happened to many people when approaching the coast with bad visibility, the mark may not be found. When this happens, there are two courses of action to take. Firstly one can obtain as true an Estimated Position as possible from the plot, using compass, log, watch and lead line, then sail in the direction of the mark using all four aids. It is extraordinary how often, after taking one or two stabs at it, one usually finds the missing mark. Never expect the mark to come up first time, right on time. There are too many imponderables in navigation for this to happen often, though when it does, the navigator does get a truly wonderful feeling! I usually allow at least five minutes beyond the expected time of appearance of the mark, and then search all round the horizon very carefully. If the mark doesn't show up I refer back to the plot to see if I have made a bad mistake. If I cannot find one, I try a fresh approach beginning from the plot at the end of the last run. If this fails, I try sailing carefully a mile or two inshore, still keeping up a careful all-round search, and then listen for breakers. When these are heard, it is safe to sail up or down the coast using the lead line. Sooner or later something will turn up, even if it is only a fishing boat coming out of, or entering, harbour. Whatever it is, once recognised on the chart it gives the required information for getting into harbour. But *for goodness' sake don't try this in bad weather, or on a rock-bound coast.* In both cases the best action is to sail up and down until the fog clears, or anchor if possible – out of any shipping lane. When the fog clears, approach the coast; using chart and pilot's guide, establish your position from as far offshore as possible and then make for the harbour entrance.

Approaching a coast at night is in many ways simpler than in daylight. There are lighthouses whose loom can be seen over 10 miles before the light itself comes over the horizon, so that recognition of individual lighthouses can be made while still a long way off. I have in front of me a small-scale chart of the English Channel, and on the French coast there are seven lighthouses with light ranges of more than 20 miles between Cap

Gris Nez and Dieppe, and another six between La Pointe de Barfleur and the Casquets. On the English coast between Dungeness and St Catherine's Point there are three lighthouses, two Lanbys and the Nab Tower. Between Portland Bill and the Lizard there are six more. Since, as I have explained earlier, only one light is needed for a positive fix, both the English and French shores are well served.

Approaching a coast at night in fog is a very different kettle of fish. Under these conditions, stand well offshore, out of the shipping lanes, and wait for the fog to clear – or for daylight, since fog often disperses with the sun. On those occasions when it is necessary to go inshore to get out of a shipping lane, there can be problems, but they are reduced to a minimum aboard a well-ordered boat where the navigator knows his job. The best policy is to cut inshore at right angles to the flow of traffic and, when soundings show between 7 and 10 metres (3 to 5 fathoms), anchor. Using the lead line continually, it is possible to follow the 5-metre contour as far as the entrance to the harbour or river. This is a cold and wet business, so the leadsman should be given a spell after about half an hour. Following a particular line of soundings is a very good way of finding one's way in fog providing that a keen watch is kept on the chart for any outlying dangers. Following a depth contour and noting any change of direction is one way of maintaining a reasonably accurate plot. If a sudden deepening of the water is encountered which can be recognised on the chart, this can be as good as a fix. If there is a buoy along the route, then so much the better – and even if it is slightly offshore, there is no harm in making a short excursion to find it. I have done this more than once and been rewarded for my trouble. Any action at all, however small, which will help to give a fix in fog is worth trying. Contour sailing is not only simple, it helps to give a sense of security which, in fog, is so vital for navigator and crew. Never say that you know where you are if you don't; just say 'I'm going to find out where we are'. It is when sailing single-handed that fear of, and in, fog is at its worst, and it is then that contour sailing comes into its own, because one at least knows how much water is under the keel. It is not easy, but with practice one finds a rhythm of casting lead, reading compass, casting lead again and so on. A confident navigator works well; one who has either lost confidence or is frightened will make mistakes. Therefore, do anything which will maintain confidence, providing that it assists navigation and safety.

A great deal has been written about horizontal sextant angles as a means of obtaining a fix. Using this method from the bridge of a merchant ship or warship has a great deal to recommend it for speed and accuracy; from the deck of a small sailing cruiser it does not find very much favour with me owing to the difficulty of using a sextant on a platform which is probably bouncing about like a demented grasshopper. Getting a sun sight from the deck of a small boat is difficult enough, but taking a round of horizontal angles is often impossible. Nonetheless the method is worth looking at. I do not recommend an expensive sextant for a small boat; a light plastic one, such as the Davis series, is quite good enough and is surprisingly accurate considering its price. One other device is needed when taking a round of angles; this is an angle pointer, and though it appears similar to a woodworker's bevel is of a different construction – as shown in Fig 49. An angle is taken between two objects A and B, see Fig 50, and is set up on the angle pointer, using a compass rose for convenience. Remember

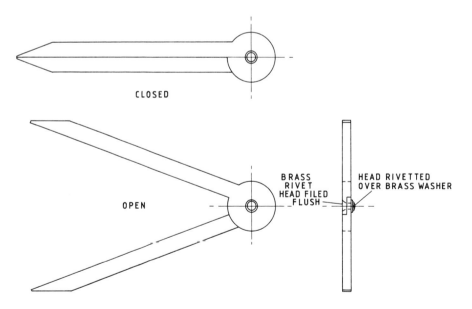

Fig 49

that this angle has no reference to the compass, and is therefore true. Let us say that this angle AOB (O being the observer) is 64°. This value is set on the pointer, one arm is placed on the chart so as to pass through A, and the other to pass through B. Since O is the observer's position, there is only one condition where the arms of the pointer can pass through A and B.

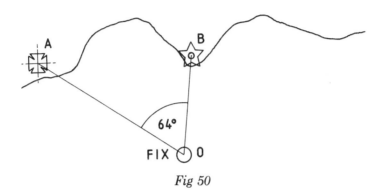

Fig 50

Another method of obtaining a fix is by measuring the angle subtended by an object of known height. The nautical almanacs give tables of distance off by vertical angle. For example, a lighthouse is shown on the chart as being 138ft 0in (42m) above the height of Least Astronomical Tide (LAT). After making the necessary adjustments for the height of tide and the height of eye of the observer, the vertical angle is measured by sextant. This angle is taken from the *top* of the *light* to sea level, as shown in Fig 51. Any necessary corrections are made for index error to give an included angle which, we will say, is 2° 36'. For a height of 138ft 0in we find that the distance off is 0.5 n miles. A bearing taken at the same time as the sextant angle will provide a bearing and range fix.

These then are the main methods of obtaining a sextant fix but, as I have said, a small boat is not an ideal platform from which to obtain accurate vertical or horizontal angles.

If, after all the care and attention to detail taken by a navigator in maintaining his Estimated Course and Positions, a mark fails to appear on schedule, there is one immediate course of action to be taken. The whole plot must be checked through for any mistakes. No mistakes must mean that there is a difference between the actual tidal stream and tidal atlas, or the mark has been moved, and this is not as unlikely as it might seem. Therefore check the tide tables and atlas for anything which may have been missed. Failing this, and being certain that the last EP was correct, alter course by 90° either way and sail for a mile on that course keeping up a constant search for the missing mark, *and keep the plot going.* If after a mile no mark appears, alter course 180° and try in the opposite direction for double the distance sailed on the last leg. If still nothing appears, carefully check the latest Notices to Mariners. Failing information from this source, the only possible step is to approach the coast with the greatest care, pick up any easily identifiable feature and fix the boat's position from it. When you are sure, and only when, set course for your destination.

Some coastlines, however, do not lend themselves to this method since they are flat and featureless, and these usually have shallow water extending for some distance offshore. In this case, sail as close in as possible, and sail along a contour until you either meet a navigation mark, or a prominent feature ashore is

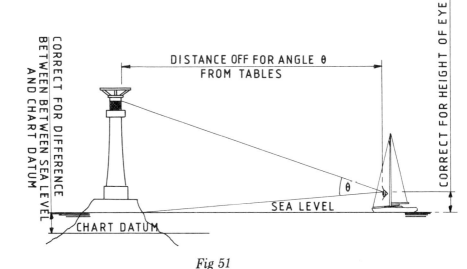

Fig 51

recognised from the chart and a fix obtained. But remember, *do not succumb to wishful thinking*; because you are hoping for a particular feature, and something like it appears, do not take it as proof that it is what you are looking for. Many boats have gone ashore through such a mistake. A careful use of compass, chart, watch and lead line, nautical almanac and pilot's guide will eventually provide proof, one way or another.

5
Electronic Equipment

It is considered by some that electronic equipment of any kind is an unnecessary luxury aboard a small boat. My opinion, backed by a number of years' experience, is that – providing that the pocket can stand the initial expense – some items, whilst not vital, can be of great help to the navigator. There are aids which it would be nice to have, but which are either too expensive or require too great a battery capacity to be practicable; radar is an example. There are makes of yacht radar which it would be quite possible to fit aboard a small cruiser, but their demand is something of the order of 50 watts which, from a normal small boat battery, would resemble a current demand of approximately 4·2 amps at 12 volts and this using a 75 ampere/hour battery and ignoring all other electrical demands, would last eighteen hours at the most without the battery receiving any charge. Using a wind- or water-driven generator with a maximum rated output of 4·5 amps, the actual input into the battery would rarely exceed 3 amps. The answer would appear to be a larger-capacity battery, but since space is at a premium aboard mini-cruisers and weight an important factor, a larger battery could present problems of its own. If, however, questions of pocket and space do not arise, I would recommend the small boat owner to fit radar. Apart from the safety aspect and the confidence it would bring, the navigator would benefit enormously. It gives an entirely different dimension to finding one's way in the dark or fog. With intelligent interpretation of the radar 'picture' a navigator can see his position and obtain a good fix either by cross bearings or by bearing and range. The modern small boat radar has an accuracy on maximum range of under 2 per cent, and this must give a navigator enormous confidence.

Whilst on the subject of radar, I feel it to be a good idea to examine the relationship between a small yacht and a merchant ship. It must first be realised that the sensitivity of the normal big ship radar is such that, whilst it will show a response from even quite small steel hulls, it can fail (as mentioned earlier) to show a recognisable or continuous response to a yacht's radar reflector. This is not due to the failure of the radar, but to the small echo produced by the reflector, too many of which are deliberately kept small to reduce windage. Also, a heeling yacht can dip her reflector below the radar 'lobe', see Fig 28 (ii), p 62, and radar aerials and reflectors are not always rigged in the optimum position and attitude. Consequently the response as shown on the screen could well be mistaken for wave clutter which, unless the set is fitted with an anti-clutter device, could well blank out a radar-reflector response. It must also be realised that some ships have quite large blind areas forward because the lobe is cut off, or just does not reach sea level soon enough, Fig 28 (i). Another factor in the recognition of yachts on big ship radars is that the set is not usually continuously manned except aboard naval vessels. Consequently the officer of the watch, taking his periodic look at the PPI Tube, may well not recognise a small 'break' as anything but local clutter, or he may miss it completely. I have never, even aboard quite big boats, relied upon being 'seen', and have made decisions on that basis. Even the best radar reflectors, such as the Firdell, cannot, through no fault of the equipment, be relied upon to make a big ship realise that there is another vessel in the vicinity. This is as a result of some or all of the factors mentioned above.

Fortunately it is possible to use another ship's radar emissions to give reasonably accurate information as to whether risk of collision exists or not. There are radar detectors on the market which will give a bearing on the origin of a radar signal. Because it is impossible for a radar detector to measure the time taken for a signal to reach the yacht from its point of origin, it cannot tell how far away that point is, but it is possible to tell from which point of the compass it is coming. If the angle remains more or less constant a risk of collision exists; if it changes by a measurable amount, one has to judge by the rate of change whether or not the ship will pass with a good margin of safety. If there is the least doubt, assume that a risk of collision exists and alter course accordingly. I am assuming that conditions of fog or low visibility exist. If a navigator finds himself approaching a shipping lane, particularly one of high density, he must keep out if possible, and keep using the radar detector; there may be a rogue about.

The way to use most radar detectors is as follows (two people are better than one for this, one to operate the detector and one to log the readings). It is easiest to assume that your own boat is stationary for plotting purposes, and to use a plotting sheet, as shown in Fig 52. Hold the detector in the upright position to check if there are any radar signals to receive. If there are, change the detector to the horizontal position, and rotate it in a clockwise direction. As each signal comes up, call out its bearing to the plotter who enters it with a prefix letter and number on the plotting sheet, as in Fig 53. The radar detector I used had a compass attachment which, although it behaved consistently, may not have been a very good idea. I see no objection to taking bearings from the ship's head since all bearings are relative to the boat. Consequently, if one takes a set of bearings relative to the ship's head, a change of bearing or a continuous one will show.

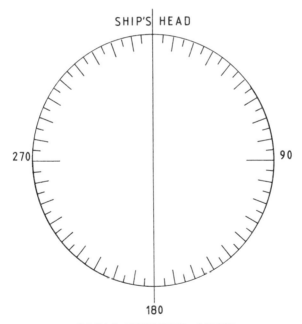

RADAR DETECTOR SHEET

Fig 52

Therefore, for use with the latest radar detectors, which have no compass fitted, I have designed a form of Pelorus with the ship's head as 0°. It is simply a Perspex disc with a fore-and-aft line (0° and 180°). The athwartships line (90° and 270°) is also marked. The edge is graduated in 10° and 5° angles as shown in Fig 54. A hole is drilled through the centre of the disc through which is mounted a carriage for the detector which is free to rotate, and an arm with a pointer is attached to it which must be parallel to the antenna of the set. The underside of the Perspex is painted white to make the graduations show up clearly. The whole system is firmly mounted in a position where it can be read easily. As the set rotates, a signal is received and its bearing recorded. Whilst this is in progress the helmsman must maintain as steady a course as possible, and call out any variation over 2° so that a correction can be made on the plotting sheet. Any variation anti-clockwise should be called out as *plus* so that the recorder can add the

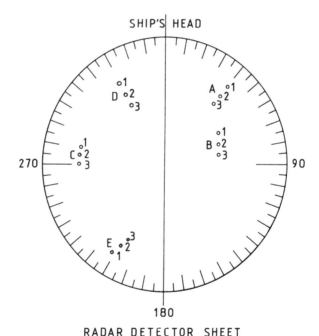

RADAR DETECTOR SHEET

Fig 53

112

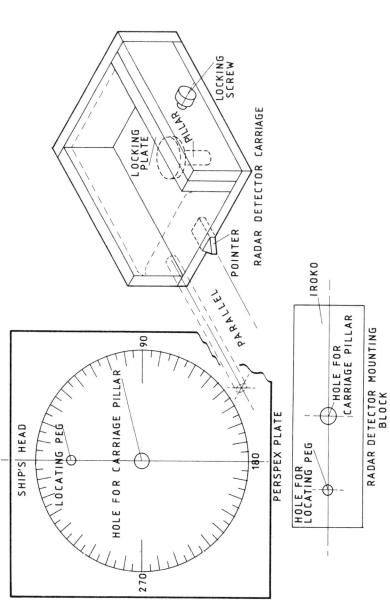

LOCKING SCREW

LOCKING PLATE

PILLAR

RADAR DETECTOR CARRIAGE

POINTER

PARALLEL

90

SHIP'S HEAD

LOCATING PEG

HOLE FOR CARRIAGE PILLAR

180

270

PERSPEX PLATE

IROKO

HOLE FOR CARRIAGE PILLAR

HOLE FOR LOCATING PEG

RADAR DETECTOR MOUNTING BLOCK

Fig 54

correction. Likewise any clockwise variation should be called out as *minus*. This method may seem complicated, but with very little practice it becomes simple, and a reasonably accurate angular location of radar signal will be obtained. Even though consecutive signals would seem to indicate that the ship will clear the yacht, it should continue to be logged on the recording sheet just in case it changes course. There are no range rings on the plotting sheet; the displacements shown in Fig 53 are to differentiate between successive plots. If no signals are received after a careful scan, the detector can be put away for ten minutes because even a ship travelling at 30 knots (unlikely in fog) will have made only 5 miles and her radar signal would probably be received in excess of this. One final point: even though a radar detector is carried and used, the normal procedures for sailing in fog should still be employed because it is quite possible that a ship's radar is out of action. Radar detectors are not all that expensive, and will repay their cost in the added peace of mind they will give.

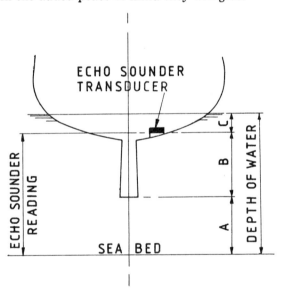

A   DEPTH TO UNDER SIDE OF KEEL
B   FACE OF TRANSDUCER TO UNDER SIDE
    OF KEEL
C   FACE OF TRANSDUCER TO SEA LEVEL

Fig 55

114

Taking an all-round look at the electronic equipment available to yachtsmen, price should not be the only consideration, although it will obviously be of great importance. My opinion is that function is the prime factor after which cost has to be considered. Cruising area and type of cruising ground are additional considerations. For the man whose cruising is limited to estuaries with occasional hops along the coast I would recommend an echo sounder as first choice, and the question to be answered is 'which is the best one I can afford?' Since most mini-cruisers sail in comparatively shallow water, I would suggest that the simplest type obtainable is quite adequate. The second question is whether to have the instrument calibrated in feet/fathoms or metres. Since practically all new editions of charts are being published with soundings in metres, my choice would be for the metric calibration with an alarm facility.

To use an echo sounder to its fullest potential requires practice, but most important is to install it correctly in exact accordance with the manufacturer's instructions. The best electronic instruments, of whatever type or make, will not perform with perfection unless correctly installed. After fitting an echo sounder, go out for a sail, switch it on and watch how the depth of water changes as shown on the display. But always remember that the recorded depth is that from the transducer to the bottom, NOT from the waterline or from the deepest part of the keel, see Fig 55. It is possible to check the exactness of the instrument by using an accurately marked lead line in still water and comparing the results, not forgetting to make allowance for the distance between the face of the transducer and the waterline. Any small differences can be corrected by the calibration knob on the set. The makers of most echo sounders give an accuracy figure of about plus or minus 2 per cent so, if, in making adjustments to the calibration, it is found to be more than this, the set should be returned to the manufacturer. However, it is very rare indeed that this is found to be necessary.

Having satisfied yourself that the equipment is working correctly, take a local large-scale chart and go to an area where there are a number of significantly different soundings, and watch how these are shown up on the display. If the sounder is fitted with a shallow water alarm, sail inshore with the alarm set at 2 feet (0.6 metres) over draught of the boat, again measured from the face of the transducer allowing for the distance to the underside of the keel. As you move into shallower water you will see the depth getting less until indicator and alarm spots correspond when the alarm will sound.

Once you have got used to the changing depths on the indicator, and have gained some experience in the behaviour of the sea-bed, it is time to move on to the more subtle use of the echo sounder. One element of this is contour sailing which I mentioned in the previous chapter. With practice this can prove to be one of the most useful ways in which to use an echo sounder. Contour sailing consists of sailing through water at constant depth. This can be, with the aid of a chart, an accurate and safe system of finding one's way into an estuary in bad visibility or at night. There are two methods of contour sailing: one can, from the chart, choose a depth which will keep one clear of outlying dangers, or one can follow a chart contour line such as the 5-metre or 5-fathom lines. Using the first method, a depth is chosen which gives plenty of water under the keel and which, by checking on the chart, keeps the boat clear of all dangers. Suppose that we choose to have 3 metres under the keel; we have to add the depth of the keel below the transducer, which we will assume to be just under 1 metre. Therefore we aim to sail keeping the depth indicator at 4 metres. The advantage of using this method is that we don't have to make any calculations to allow for the height of the tide. The disadvantage is that an accurate plot has to be maintained on the chart, so that the actual position of the boat over the ground, Estimated Position, actual course sailed and Estimated Course shall be as close as possible to each other. A fair check can be made by calculating the actual depth of water, allowing for the state of the tide, at an EP. If the calculated depth corresponds fairly closely with the depth on the indicator, this can be accepted as a reasonably accurate check. Following a contour line on the chart is possibly easier to do, but it calls for hourly checks on actual depth in relation to the height of the tide. By taking advantage of sudden changes in the direction of a contour line, it is possible to get a fix for position.

When contour sailing, the bias, if any, should always be towards the deeper water, thus giving a slight advantage should something unforeseen happen. A man I know, while contour sailing, once ran full tilt into an unlit and uncharted buoy, fortunately without doing any damage. As he so very rightly remarked later, 'That'll teach me to keep a proper look-out'. Do not, because you are sailing on an echo sounder, neglect the dictates᾽ of good seamanship. This, as with all electronic instruments, is an aid to navigation only. All the requirements of seamanship and good navigation must continue.

Contour sailing can also be used for finding one's way along a channel in a river or estuary that is badly buoyed. I always recommend newcomers to the ownership of an echo sounder to practise this, and to try sailing in different depths of water. When one has had plenty of practice in the general method try sailing with half a metre or less under the keel. My reason for recommending this is that ability to sail in shallow water, without running on and off the bottom, means that, in fog, one can sail in shallow water out of the main channel, thereby reducing the chances of a collision.

The last, but by no means least important, method of using an echo sounder is profile sailing. Anyone who has learnt map reading on land will know how to produce the profile of a line across country. The same can be done with a chart to produce a profile of the sea-bed. By this means it is possible to check whether an Estimated Course is actually being sailed. I am not going to pretend that the method is simple, or that it can be done quickly. It requires time, patience and a small amount of drawing ability. There are two methods: one can prepare the profile for a planned course and compare this with what actually unfolds, or a profile can be prepared from a set of previous echo-sounder readings as entered in the navigation log, and compared with the chart until one finds a line which corresponds. In either case one really has to draw two profiles on the same piece of paper initially, but with experience it is possible to tell whether or not the drawn profile agrees with the sounding figures on the chart.

Profiles produced from echo-sounder readings have to be reduced to Chart Datum Sea Level, otherwise they will be false, because while the boat sails through the water this will be growing shallower or deeper according to the changing state of the tide. When an appreciable difference between two profiles is noticed, it is possible to tell which way to turn to get back on course through the change in the style of the profile; perhaps it starts to drop suddenly when it should have been going up slowly, or vice versa.

This should show on the chart, and the necessary course correction be made.

The way to draw a profile is simply a matter of common sense allied to an ability to draw a graph; there is only one difference – the zero line is at the top of the paper because the horizontal datum line represents sea level to Chart Datum, and it is depths below this level which are recorded. The vertical scale is chosen to cover the entire range of depths to be encountered on the course

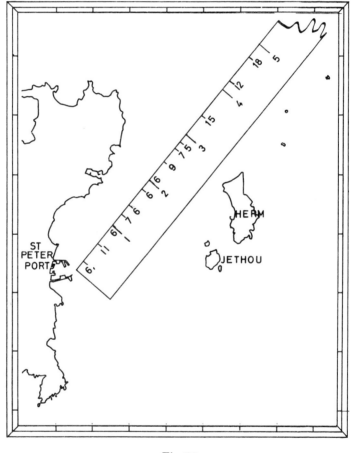

Fig 56

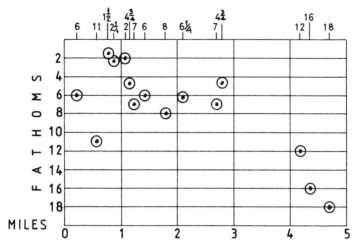

HORIZONTAL SCALE: 32mm to 1n mile
VERTICAL SCALE: 5mm to 1fathom

Fig 57

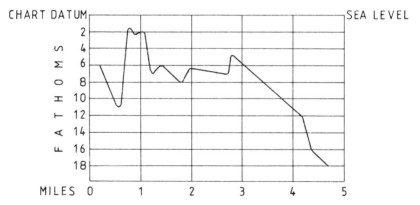

HORIZONTAL SCALE: 32mm to 1n mile
VERTICAL SCALE: 5mm to 1fathom

PROFILE OF SEABED IN LITTLE RUSSEL CHANNEL

Fig 58

119

sailed, and should be as small as is practicable to show clearly the alterations in depth. The horizontal scale along the top of the sheet must be that of the chart in use, and for this reason there is little or no point in using small-scale charts. A natural scale of about 1:50,000 is about the smallest; anything smaller would not give much of a profile. Having chosen a suitable vertical scale, the horizontal one being that of the chart in use, a reference point, such as the last positive fix, is chosen. The edge of the paper is laid along the proposed course and the distances and depths of all soundings are marked along it, see Fig 56. The soundings are marked in *below* the horizontal datum line as in Fig 57; a dot with a ring round it is the best way of doing this. When the required distance has been covered and the dots are joined up, a profile of the sea-bed, exaggerated because of the vertical scale, has been obtained, see Fig 58. Remember that all soundings taken from the chart are below chart datum, which on the newer British charts is the Lowest Astronomical Tide (LAT), and on older charts Mean Low Water Springs (MLWS). It is as well, therefore, to check the chart in use and to remember that, since new tide tables are based on LAT, there will be a small difference if the chart datum is MLWS. This will result in the calculated depth being slightly

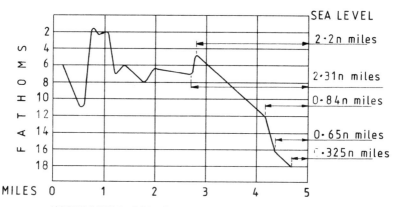

PROFILE OF SEABED IN LITTLE RUSSEL CHANNEL

Fig 59

greater than that shown on the echo sounder. To compare the plotted profile with that over which one is sailing, the echosounder readings will have to have two corrections: one for the height difference between waterline and transducer, and the other the difference between actual and charted depth. The latter correction, based upon the state of the tide, can be calculated by using the 'Rule of Twelfths', which is a good general approximation, and suitable for this purpose. The Rule states that the tide rises or falls:

One-twelfth of its range during the first hour
Two-twelfths of its range during the second hour (1/6)
Three-twelfths of its range during the third hour (1/4)
Three-twelfths of its range during the fourth hour (1/4)
Two-twelfths of its range during the fifth hour (1/6)
One-twelfth of its range during the sixth hour.

If one wants to be really accurate, one uses the tidal curves, a description of which is rather too lengthy for this little book. A very good explanation is to be found in the *Macmillan Silk Cut Nautical Almanac*. As the boat sails along, readings are taken from the echo sounder at intervals which correspond with the distances apart of the points on the profile drawing, see Fig 59. I have not given all the distances, for the sake of clarity, but the drawing does illustrate the principle. Thus, one person keeps an eye on the log and, when the required distance comes up, the sounding is read off; then, after making the two necessary corrections, it is transferred to the drawing. If the boat is on course, the profile and recorded soundings should be very similar. It is unlikely that they will coincide exactly because the actual depth of water and that which is calculated are very rarely the same, mainly because of wind effect but also because of the boat's position on a wave at the moment of recording the sounding. With light winds and small waves there should be very little difference; what there is will probably be due to the fact that the tides do not always behave as predicted.

With stronger winds and bigger waves, differences could be over a metre. The wind affects the tides. A strong wind against tide will tend to hold the water back, whereas wind and tide together could mean that the tides in some areas will be higher or lower than predicted, see Fig 60. The time may come when a large discrepancy shows up on the profile sheet, and the navigator has to decide which side of his planned course the boat has gone. Since he may be sailing in conditions of visibility which either prevent him from seeing the coast, or prevent him from seeing it clearly enough to obtain a fix, he has but one resort: the chart. With one to a reasonably large scale he might be able to pinpoint the cause of the discrepancy, because of an odd sounding or a steeply shelving bank which has turned up sooner or later than expected – this is shown at point X in Fig 61. By the time he is within half a mile of the harbour entrance, he is about $1\frac{1}{2}$ cables to the south of his course, and must alter accordingly. If there is no actual indication from the chart the navigator has to make an intelligent guess as to the right course to take, and this is where experience tells. But, if he is approaching a coast, he would do better to change over to contour sailing.

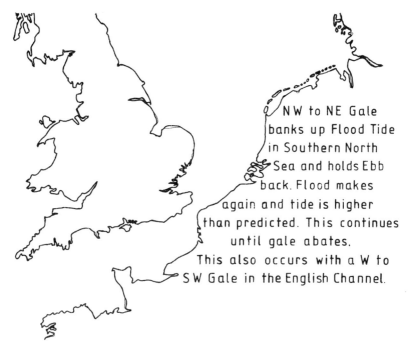

NW to NE Gale banks up Flood Tide in Southern North Sea and holds Ebb back. Flood makes again and tide is higher than predicted. This continues until gale abates.
This also occurs with a W to SW Gale in the English Channel.

Fig 60

The second method of profile sailing is used when the navigator does not know where he is when approaching a coast. If he has maintained echo-sounder readings in his navigation log – which, when approaching a coast, he should do anyway – the profile which these produce, corrected to chart datum, can be compared with the chart and an approximation of position obtained when chart and profile correspond. This is not a method I like, and I hardly ever use it.

A more expensive type of echo sounder records soundings continuously on paper from a roll, and this saves time in having to draw a profile. Where the speed of recording is adjustable, it is possible with considerable practice to produce a profile to chart scale.

Next to an echo sounder, in order of priority, I would place a Radio Direction Finding (RDF) set. Day or night, clear or fog, an RDF set is a boon to the navigator. But be warned; any RDF set, cheap or expensive, if not used intelligently or correctly can be a menace because more reliance will be placed on it than is warranted. But in good hands it will give as good results as can be

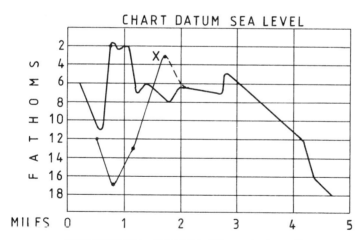

HORIZONTAL SCALE: 32mm to 1n mile
VERTICAL SCALE: 5mm to 1 fathom
PROFILE OF SEABED IN LITTLE RUSSEL CHANNEL

Fig 61

asked for. The system is perfectly simple, calling only for the set itself, a reliable watch and the identification signal, mode and timing of the beacon being sought. All this information is obtainable from the nautical almanacs, and any alterations are published in the Notices to Mariners, and repeated in some yachting journals. There are two important requirements for the RDF-set operator: the first is positive aural recognition of the Morse Code, and the second is practice in the use of the set. It must be obvious that without the former an RDF set is useless, and that for the latter all that is needed is time and patience in getting to know the set and how to use it. No specialised teaching is required; just follow the instructions in the manual and you can teach yourself. Aural recognition of the Morse Code requires practice. When learning the Code it is, in my experience, useless to learn the letters by dot and dash; learn them by saying 'dit' for the dots and 'dah' for the dashes so that the sound of each letter is learnt. When the time comes to put it into practice, the recognition of individual letters is much easier. An example of what I mean is shown in Fig 62 (see also p138). Having learnt the Code, try to get hold of a key-operated electric buzzer (cheap to buy or make) and enlist the help of a friend, preferably one who knows Morse Code, to send the letters. The friend will probably need a bit of practice, will learn the Code if he doesn't already know it, and help you to perfect your recognition of it. When you can receive the Morse Code at about fifteen letters a minute you will be able to recognise the identification signals of radio

LETTER	MORSECODE	SOUND
A	• ▬	DIT DAH
C	▬ • ▬ •	DAH DIT DAH DIT
F	• • ▬ •	DIT DIT DAH DIT
M	▬ ▬	DAH DAH
Q	▬ ▬ • ▬	DAH DAH DIT DAH
V	• • • ▬	DIT DIT DIT DAH

Fig 62

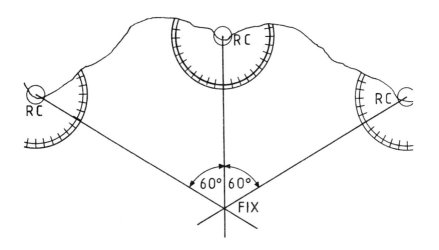

Fig 63

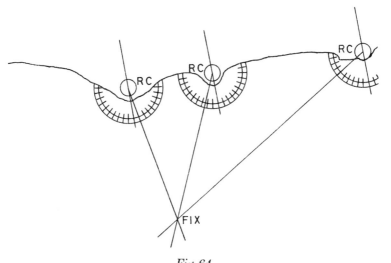

Fig 64

beacons without difficulty. Learning the Morse Code is a good winter evening occupation; an alternative way of learning to self-teaching is to attend those evening classes which give instruction to amateur wireless enthusiasts who have to be able to send and receive Morse by key in order to obtain their operating licences.

Once the Morse Code has been learnt, the RDF set can be used. The best way to get plenty of practice is to take the set every time you go sailing, and use it to obtain bearings either on radio beacons, aero radio beacons or even on normal broadcasting stations which cover your area. As I said before, the method is quite simple. Write down the names of the nearest beacons with their frequency, identification signals, modes and timing sequence. All these are obtainable from the nautical almanacs. Choose one of these, tune to its frequency, and at the time it is due to transmit you will hear its signal. If you don't hear it, turn the tuning dial slightly either way and you should pick it up. This of course does not apply to those sets equipped with push-button tuning. When the identification signal stops it will be followed by a long dash. The set is rotated until a minimum signal or 'nul' is received, when the bearing is noted. The same procedure is carried out for at least two other beacons. The ideal cut between any two stations is 60°, see Fig 63. However, this is not always possible, but whatever the bearing the navigator, taking each beacon in turn, converts it into a back bearing which is laid off on the chart using the compass rose drawn on the chart round the beacon. This is done for each beacon in turn, and ideally the point where the three lines cross is the boat's position, see Fig 64. It is seldom, however, that the three lines make a perfect cross; the more usual result is a small triangle, the famous 'cocked hat'. The size of the cocked hat gives some idea of the accuracy of the bearings obtained. Obviously a large triangle must be treated with reservation, a small one accepted – the boat's position being at the centre of the triangle. If the triangle is large, the bearings should be checked again and, if there was a measurable interval between obtaining each one (anything over five minutes), a correction must be made for the change of position of the yacht. If after this correction the triangle is still large, take a fresh round of angles and start again. By using the Mark V chart board and A3 size charts, duly modified, the time taken in producing the yacht's position is very much reduced when comparing the same function using a folded chart on the knees. After many years' experience of using RDF sets held in the hand, I still get cocked hats, and in fact very seldom get a perfect cross; like a good many experienced navigators I tend to be suspicious of one, and then render thanks to Neptune, Poseidon and all the nautical deities I can think of. So, if after considerable practice you still haven't obtained that much-sought-after cross, don't be downhearted.

A great many factors can affect the quality of RDF bearings, not least of which are atmospheric conditions. These can bend a beam sufficiently for the bearing to be well off on occasions. Also, a bearing taken over land where the line to the beacon is not at right angles to the coast will be refracted and give a false reading. Other factors are whether or not it was taken near the limit of range of the beacon, or whether the set was used an hour before or after sunrise or sunset. Using a small hand-held RDF set, I would not employ a beacon at more than 75 per cent of its range. For instance, the Round Island Beacon in the Isles of Scilly has a published range of up to 200 miles; I would not use it at a greater range than 150 miles, and would certainly never use it if I had closed the beacon with the Land's End peninsula. The beacon at St Catherine's Point on the Isle of Wight can be trusted practically all the way across the Channel to the Cherbourg peninsula because there is no land for it to cross, and the signal seems reasonably accurate up to 40 miles. If only two beacons appear to be within decent range, one can take two bearings to obtain a preliminary fix, and then take a running fix on one or the other – preferably the one furthest along the course being sailed.

Obtaining any kind of bearing aboard a small boat in a seaway will not be as accurate as the plus or minus half a degree of which a small hand-held RDF set is capable. Under some circumstances one will be very lucky to get within plus or minus three degrees!

There arises the question of discrepancies between an Estimated Position obtained by careful plotting of the course being sailed by log and compass, and an RDF fix. A good navigator will compare a series of the two taken over a period of at least some hours to see if the difference continues. Finally, after weighing up all the evidence at his disposal, he has to make a decision as to which of the two is the most likely to be correct. A great deal depends upon beacon range and atmospheric conditions, particularly if there are thunderstorms about. Under reasonable conditions I prefer to trust my RDF fixes, but I make sure that I calculate my next EP from the last one, and also from the next EP from the last RDF fix. From the results I can usually tell which of the two I can rely on. In Fig 65, the navigator has plotted his Estimated Course through EP1 to EP2 and EP3. He maintained this course to windward and up tide of his planned course into the mouth of the estuary. He made, in my opinion, two errors; fortunately neither of them very large. The first was that he did not make a sufficient allowance for tide. Since wind (Force 4) and tide were together, the rate of tidal flow would be more than shown in the tidal atlas, and surface drift should have been allowed for. The second mistake came in not trusting his RDF set enough. His first two fixes should have shown him that he was to leeward of both his Planned and Estimated Courses, and he should have altered course when RF2 proved this. As it was, he only realised the truth at RF3, by which time he had to alter course to make allowance for the tide in order to pass close to starboard of the leading port-hand buoy since the channel in the very small mouth of the estuary was itself very narrow. This resulted in the boat having to come hard on the wind for the last 12 miles or so of what had been a long and tiring sail.

The navigator aboard a yacht outward bound from Salcombe

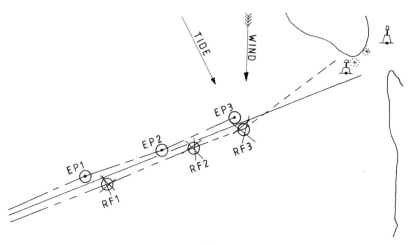

Fig 65

decided two things at the start. Firstly that the trip would take twelve hours to a point 3 miles west of Les Hanois Light, and secondly that he could therefore, quite legitimately, assume that the tides would cancel out. As the passage progressed he found that his RDF fixes were moving to the West of his Estimated Course. After about eight hours the fixes had reduced their westward tendency, returned back across the Estimated Course, and were then to the eastward of it. In other words, the RDF fixes had shown the amount of tidal effect on both ebb and flood. I reproduce the trace here in Fig 66. This bears out my tendency to trust my RDF fixes unless I am given very good reason to doubt

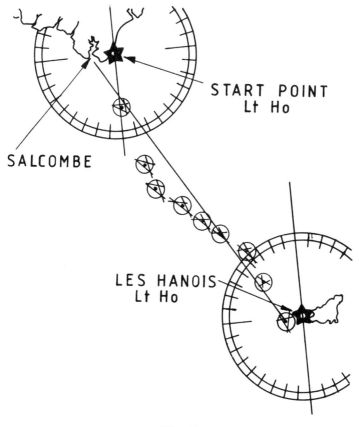

Fig 66

them. This might appear to be a dangerous generalisation, but some years' experience has gone into giving me this trust. After all, what is the sense in spending good money on an item of navigation equipment if you are not going to trust it. I have to admit that it took me some time before I believed it to be really trustworthy. At the present state of the art in electronics, hand-held RDF sets are very reliable. To endorse my belief in small RDF sets still more, I will here state that I have not had to swim for my life as a result of an error in my navigation . . . YET!

All round the coasts of the British Isles and Europe there are a number of aero radio beacons which are for the purpose of assisting in aircraft navigation. They are shown on charts by the letters ARC in magenta. The yachtsman also can use them, and one often finds that a better cut can be obtained from one of these than from a marine radio beacon. Aero radio beacons *which are near the coast* give accurate bearings; all have individual identification signals and similar modes to their marine counterparts, but there is one big difference: they transmit continuously. This last factor makes them of great use to us providing that they are close to the coastline so that they are not affected by land refraction. The ones which are reliable in this sense are shown on most charts. Identification signals and so forth are given in the nautical almanacs.

One last word about RDF equipment, and this applies to all electronic equipment carried aboard small cruisers. Take great care of it if you wish it to retain its efficiency. A hand-held set must *never* be left lying on a cockpit seat. Most of them are supplied with a stowage bracket, and this should be fixed in a dry part of the ship away from any danger of being knocked and damaged. The best practice is to send all electronic instruments back to the manufacturers for servicing at least once every two years; better, annually. Also, in view of the enormous amount of theft from boats these days, removable items of equipment should, if possible, be taken home when not in use, and all items should be individually insured for their replacement value so that, in the event of theft, they can be replaced as quickly as possible. Another security device is to mark your Post Code in special ink on each item of equipment. The local Crime Prevention Officer will be only too pleased to advise on this matter.

There is the question of the uses of VHF radio to the navigator to

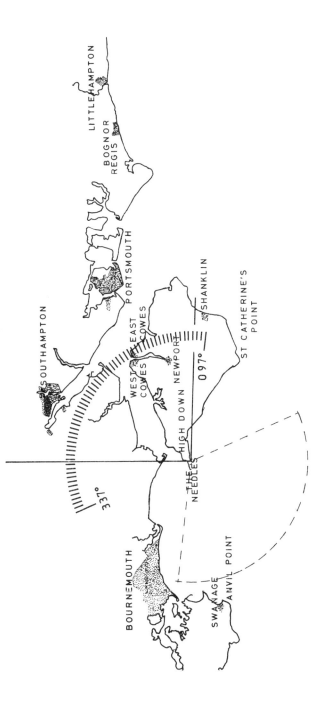

HIGH DOWN, SCRATCHELLS BAY VHF RADIO LIGHTHOUSE
RANGE: 20 n.miles   Position: 50° 39'42"N 1° 34'36"W.
Calibrated 337° to 097°
SEA AREA COVERED BY SIGNALS SHOWN BY DOTTED SEGMENT OF CIRCLE

Fig 67

be answered. I think that its foremost role must be that of safety. All good navigators should be interested in safety, not only for their own vessel, but for all those within range. VHF Channel 16 is the distress and calling frequency and all ships, including yachts, are encouraged to listen in on this channel. A distress call is preceded by the code word MAYDAY repeated three times, and it has priority over all other types of call. It is the duty of anyone receiving a MAYDAY call to wait one minute to find out if the call is answered by the rescue authorities or another ship. If no reply is received, the yacht receiving the call should broadcast a MAYDAY RELAY call. Upon being answered, he passes the original message and then stands by in case his services are required to act as a relay station or to go to the assistance of the vessel in distress if this is at all practicable. It is important that the navigator plots the position of the vessel in trouble, and works out his best course to get to him. It is the unwritten law of the sea that we all, yachtsmen included, go to each other's assistance; there is no excuse for failing to do so once it is known that another vessel in the vicinity is in need of help.

Channel 16 is also used for urgent signals prefaced by the code words PAN PAN. This type of message concerns the safety of a person or vessel, and its priority is second only to a MAYDAY call. Again, a yacht receiving this message must do all in her power to be of assistance. The code word SÉCURITÉ precedes important messages relating to the safety of navigation, and is usually broadcast by a coast radio station. Also, a SÉCURITÉ call can be initiated by a ship to warn all other shipping of a hazard to navigation such as a mark adrift or out of position or, of more immediate interest to small boats, floating dangers such as a container washed off a ship and floating half submerged. This latter could be fatal to a small cruiser should she hit it, and it is the navigator's job to mark its last reported position and probable direction and rate of drift on his chart. From this information he can assess whether or not the hazard is likely to be a danger to his boat and, if so, what action to take to avoid it. All MAYDAY, PAN PAN and SÉCURITÉ calls *must be entered* in the yacht's radio log, as well as any action taken, which should also be entered in the yacht's log.

An additional service, one which is supplied by Trinity House for the VHF user, is the new series of VHF radio lighthouses. Up until the time of their introduction, there was no means by which it was possible to obtain a fix using VHF radio. Now, with the introduction of these lighthouses, this is possible. Each lighthouse broadcasts on Channel 88 and gives a frequency modulated signal. Some have a range of up to 30 miles, whilst others can only reach out to about 14 miles. The lighthouses work in pairs, and can be used to obtain a crossing fix, whilst a single one can be used for a running fix. Fig 67 shows that the High Down VHF Radio Lighthouse is calibrated from 337° True to 097° True and, working on normal RDF practice, one would suppose that the area covered would be part of Hampshire, the Solent and part of the Isle of Wight. This of course is wrong. The VHF signal one receives from these lighthouses is a reciprocal of the bearings shown on my drawing, so that what actually happens is that the signal is received as a back bearing and, when the 'nul' comes up, the bearing obtained is that of the lighthouse *from* the vessel. That is why Fig 67 shows a dotted quadrant with its two extremities as reciprocals of the two limits of calibration. All one has to do is to count the number of beats heard until the 'nul' comes up. By referring to the tables published for that particular lighthouse, the bearing from the boat to the lighthouse is read off, and laid off on the chart. By repeating this for an associated lighthouse, in the case of High Down it is Anvil Point, it is possible to obtain a two-bearing fix. It must always be remembered, however, that bearings from VHF radio lighthouses are only accurate *to plus or minus 2°* and this is regardless of range so that the fix obtained will only be to that order of accuracy.

Never try to home directly on to a radio lighthouse. Steer to one side or the other, and take a series of running fixes, but always bear in mind the limits of accuracy, and keep well away from outlying dangers; in the case of High Down these would be the Needles to the West, and St Catherine's Point to the East. As experience in using VHF radio lighthouses grows, the navigator's confidence in them will grow also, and he will become more and more confident of the fixes he obtains from them.

What has been written in this book is from hard-earned knowledge gained over the years. Nevertheless, I am the first to admit that many of the ideas and methods I have descibed can be argued about and disagreed with. You may well, in the light of experience, come to disagree with some of the things I have written, but I would ask you to remember this: the way we all live our lives is based upon past experience, and no two people's lives are exactly the same. This applies also to sailing and navigation, and is one of the fascinating aspects of our sport. I learnt to sail and to navigate on the East Coast among the sand and mudbanks of its estuaries and coast. I now live in Cornwall, and the past ten years of sailing in this area have taught me many new things, and have caused me to modify some of my thinking, especially where navigation is concerned. You can afford, at times, to run aground on mud or sand, but you can never afford to hit a rock!

Acknowledgements

John Donne wrote that 'No man is an Island of itself'. This is true of life itself in general, but in writing a book on navigation, or any other specialised subject for that matter, it is doubly true. But for the help I have received from outside sources, I would never have been able to get beyond the first two chapters. In particular I want to thank Tom Wilson Esq of Imray, Laurie, Norrie & Wilson Ltd, and Roger Hunter Esq of Barnacle Marine Ltd for their invaluable assistance on the subject of their charts and publications. Also, my grateful thanks to Monsieur Claude Vergnot, not only for the help given on the publications of Éditions Cartographiques Maritimes, but for understanding my French! My very deep gratitude goes to the Managing Director of Offshore Instruments Ltd for his great generosity in the matter of the Mini-Compass. I would also thank Seafarer Navigation International Ltd for the help given on the subject of their products. To my friend Bernard Lilley I say a most heartfelt thank you for his help with the Mark V Pantograph. To Peter and Michelle Clark, for the loan of their wonderful electric typewriter which so expertly covered up my many typing errors, thank you both very much.

R.M.T.

Useful Addresses

Seafarer and Seafix Range of Electronic Equipment:
Seafarer International Ltd, Fleets Lane, Poole, Dorset BH15 3BW

Charts and Navigation Publications:
Imray, Laurie, Norrie & Wilson Ltd, Wych House, The Broadway, St Ives, Huntingdon, Cambs PE17 4BT
Stanford Maritime Ltd, 12–14 Long Acre, London WC2E 9LP
Barnacle Marine Ltd, The Warehouse, Next to 1 Crowhurst Road, Colchester, Essex CO3 3JN*
Éditions Cartographiques Maritimes, 9 quai de l'Artois, 94170 le Perreux-sur-Marne, FRANCE
Macmillan Silk Cut Nautical Almanac, Room 412, Macmillan Press Limited, Houndmills, Basingstoke, Hampshire RG21 2XS

Cruising Association Handbook:
Cruising Association, Ivory House, St Catherine Dock, London E1 9AY

Brown's and Reed's Nautical Almanacs:
From Yacht Chandlers and Bookshops

*The publication of Stanford's Charts was taken over by Barnacle Marine Ltd in 1983.

Beaufort Scale of Wind Force

Beaufort Number	Description	Speed in knots*	Height of sea in feet†	Deep sea criteria
0	Calm	less than 1	—	Sea mirror-smooth.
1	Light air	1–3	$\frac{1}{2}$	Small wavelets like scales, no crests.
2	Light breeze	4–6	$\frac{1}{2}$	Small wavelets still short but more pronounced. Crests glassy and do not break.
3	Gentle breeze	7–10	2	Large wavelets. Crests begin to break. Foam is glassy.
4	Moderate breeze	11–16	$3\frac{1}{2}$	Small waves becoming longer; more frequent white horses.
5	Fresh breeze	17–21	6	Moderate waves, and longer; many white horses.
6	Strong breeze	22–27	$9\frac{1}{2}$	Large waves begin to form; white crests more extensive.
7	Near gale	28–33	$13\frac{1}{2}$	Sea heaps up; white foam blown in streaks.
8	Gale	34–40	18	Moderately high waves of greater length; crests begin to form spin-drift. Foam blown in well-marked streaks.
9	Strong gale	41–47	23	High waves; dense streaks of foam. Crests begin to roll over.
10	Storm	48–55	29	Very high waves with long overhanging crest. Surface of sea becomes white with great patches of foam. Visibility affected.
11	Violent storm	56–63	37	Exceptionally high waves. Sea completely covered with foam.
12	Hurricane	64+		The air is filled with spray and visibility seriously affected.

* Measured at a height of 33 feet above sea-level
† In the open sea remote from land

The Morse Code

The Morse Code should be learned by treating it as a series of sounds, not symbols. Thus B should be learned as 'dah-di-di-dit', not 'dash-dot-dot-dot'. Note that the final 't' of 'dit' is only sounded at the end of a letter code.

Letter	Code	Sound
A	.—	di-dah
B	—...	dah di-di-dit
C	—.—.	dah-di dah-dit
D	—..	dah di-dit
E	.	dit
F	..—.	di-di dah-dit
G	——.	dah-dah-dit
H	....	di-di-di-dit
I	..	di-dit
J	.———	di dah-dah-dah
K	—.—	dah-di-dah
L	.—..	di-dah di-dit
M	——	dah-dah
N	—.	dah-dit
O	———	dah-dah-dah
P	.——.	di-dah dah-dit
Q	——.—	dah-dah di-dah
R	.—.	di-dah-dit
S	...	di-di-dit
T	—	dah
U	..—	di-di-dah
V	...—	di-di-di-dah
W	.——	di dah-dah
X	—..—	dah di-di-dah
Y	—.——	dah-di dah-dah
Z	——..	dah-dah di-dit

Number	Code	Sound
1	.————	di dah-dah-dah-dah
2	..———	di-di dah-dah-dah
3	...——	di-di-di dah-dah
4	....—	di-di-di-di dah
5	.....	di-di-di-di-dit
6	—....	dah di-di-di-dit
7	——...	dah-dah di-di-dit
8	———..	dah-dah-dah dit-dit
9	————.	dah-dah-dah-dah dit
0	—————	dah-dah-dah-dah-dah

Index

Index

Index

Plywood, marine-grade, 25
Point of intersection, 96, 97, 99
Polyester film, 78
Polythene bags, 46
Port operations, 61
Position, Estimated, 49, 50, 51, 76, 86, 90, 103, 106, 107, 116, 127, 128
Position fix, 95
Positive fix, 66, 77, 86
Power output (VHF radio), 59
PPI Tube (radar), 110
Practical Boat Owner, 99
Practice, necessity of, 58
Preliminary fix, 127
Profile drawing, 117, 118, 121, 122
Profile, horizontal datum line, 120
  horizontal scale, 120
  reference point, 120
  sailing, 117, 123
  of sea-bed, 117, 120, 121, 123
  vertical scale, 118, 120
Projected course, 77
Pumice powder, 26, 41

Quartz watches, 49, 67

Radar, 109
  aerials, 110
  accuracy, 109
  detector, 63, 110, 111, 112, 114
  detector carriage, 112
  emissions, 110
  'lobe', 110
  picture, 109
  reflector, 63, 110
  reflector attitude, 110
  reflector response, 110
  screen, 63, 110
  signal, angular location of, 114
Radio beacon, air, 12, 126, 130
  characteristics, 57, 99
  frequency, 57, 58, 126
  identification signal, 123, 124, 126
  marine, 12, 4, 55, 123, 126, 130
  mode, 57, 123, 126
  range of, 127
  sequence timing, 57, 58, 123, 126
  Direction Finder (RDF), 54, 56, 57, 58, 76, 101, 123, 124, 126, 127, 129, 130
  log, 86, 132
  operator's licence, 59
  receiver, 58, 59

signal charts (French), 24
stations, coastal, 58, 60
telephony, medium frequency (MF/RT), 59
telephony, VHF (VHF/RT), 59, 60, 130
transceiver, 59, 86
Radius of maximum range, 97
Range, 95, 97, 127
Range and bearing, 98
Rangefinder, 95
Range of visibility, 14, 99
  radio beacons, 127
Rate of drift, 132
RDF bearings, effect of atmospheric conditions, 127
  sunrise and sunset, 127
  fix, 128, 129
Reciprocal bearing, 56, 133
Recorded depth, 115, 121
Reed's Nautical Almanac, 45
Refraction, 55, 127, 130
Regulations, traffic-lane, 22
Representative fraction, 69, 70
Rhumb line, 79, 80, 81, 83, 97
Risk of collision, 63, 110, 117
Rocks, 99, 100
Rose, compass, 12, 70
Round Island Radio Beacon, 55, 127
Royal Navy, 95
'Rule of Twelfths', 121
Running fix, 90, 92, 93, 94, 96, 100, 127, 133
  plot, 63, 90

Safe course, 23
Safety, 59, 105, 109, 110, 132
  margin of, 110
Sandpaper, 26
Scale of Latitude, 69
Scale, margin, 14, 17, 18
Scale, natural, 69, 70
Scheme of tacks, 22
Sea-bed contours, 51
  profile of, 117, 120, 121, 123
Sea level, Chart Datum, 117, 118, 120
Sea, meteorology at, 47
  state, 51
Search and Rescue, 62
SECURITE calls, 132
Semi-Duplex mode, 60
Separation lanes, 72
Servicing of electronic equipment, 54